GW01255370

About this Learning Guide

Shmoop Will Make You a Better Lover*
*of Literature, History, Poetry, Life...

Our lively learning guides are written by experts and educators who want to show your brain a good time. Shmoop writers come primarily from Ph.D. programs at top universities, including Stanford, Harvard, and UC Berkeley.

Want more Shmoop? We cover literature, poetry, bestsellers, music, US history, civics, biographies (and the list keeps growing). Drop by our website to see the latest.

www.shmoop.com

Table of Contents

Introduction

In a Nutshell

Published sometime between 800 and 600 BC, the *Odyssey* is, along with the *Iliad*, one of the best known, and most stupendously awesome, works of ancient literature – make that *any* literature. To fully appreciate its awesomeness, you'll have to read it for yourself – Shmoop's just here to make it a smoother ride. First, though, we can fill you in on some background information.

Being an ancient epic, the *Odyssey* was originally composed in the classic oral tradition of…not being written at all. Well, at least that's what some scholars think, pointing to how the poem's use of repetition echoes that of oral poets, who used repetition as a memory aid. On the other hand, if Homer *did* compose it on paper, wouldn't it make sense for him to imitate the style of the oral poetry before him? It's your call; the jury's still out on this one. (For more information on this debate, check out our guide to the *Iliad*.) But this is missing the point. What really matters is the amazing power of Homer's poem, which you now get to experience for yourself.

On one level, the *Odyssey* is a sequel to the *Iliad* – but don't let any prejudice about sequels throw you off. Really, the two poems are more like night and day – they complement each other, and are equally great. That said, to echo Bob Dylan, the author of these poems can definitely "take the dark out of the nighttime, / and paint the daytime black." Even though the *Iliad* is all about war and suffering, it still finds time for moments of profound humanity. Meanwhile, the *Odyssey*, which is all about Odysseus's crazy adventures on his way back home from war, never lets us forget that, for him, most of those adventures involve a lot of suffering. Also, you don't have to read the *Iliad* first – the *Odyssey* itself fills you in on most of the relevant background background information, though you might want to refresh your memory of the Trojan War, if you're feeling a bit rusty. (Unfortunately, watching the movie *Troy* doesn't count.)

One more thing: if you haven't already stopped reading this introduction and picked up Homer's book, just think of all the generations of readers who have felt that the *Odyssey* speaks to them. Many of these readers have gone on to create their own, original artworks inspired by Homer's epic. In this category, you've got Virgil's epic poem the *Aeneid*; Alfred Lord Tennyson's poem "Ulysses"; James Joyce's novel, *Ulysses*; countless paintings (check out Henry Fuseli's "Odysseus in front of Scylla and Charybdis"); Cream's song "Tales of Brave Ulysses"; the Cohen Brothers' movie *O Brother, Where Art Thou?* – and the list goes on. Whether you're most interested in literature, visual art, music, or movies, you've got to read Homer's *Odyssey* to see where everybody's getting their ideas.

Why Should I Care?

Do you like stories full of adventure, danger, and suspense? How about stories set in fantastic worlds full of strange creatures like Cyclopses, witches, sirens, and gods? If so, then you're in luck, because Homer's *Odyssey* is Western literature's original adventure story, and its first

foray into the fantasy genre. If you need any proof of how much Homer's poem defined this genre, just consider the fact that we now use the *word* "odyssey" simply to mean adventure.

OK, you're thinking, so what if it's the first, that doesn't make it the best. And you're absolutely right. The real reason you should read the *Odyssey* is because it's an incredibly exciting story that also happens to contain profound reflections on heroism, love, and human life. True, all of these themes are also dealt with in Homer's *Iliad*, but the *Odyssey* puts a different spin on them. In contrast to Achilleus, the raging warrior hero of the *Iliad*, Odysseus lives by his wits as much as by his strength.

Similarly, even though the *Iliad* contains nuanced portraits of several striking women, the *Odyssey* is unique in ancient literature for its numerous strong female characters, ranging from the cunningly faithful Penelope, to the mysterious Circe and Kalypso, to Odysseus's steadfast ally Athene, the goddess of warfare and wisdom.

By presenting the full range of human experience – including death, as revealed in Odysseus's trip to the Underworld – the *Odyssey* perfectly complements the *Iliad's* concentrated focus on the experience of war. It will give you tons of stuff to think about – though you probably won't even notice, because you'll be having so much fun.

Book Summary

Years after the end of the <u>Trojan War</u>, the Greek hero Odysseus still hasn't come home to Ithaka, and many believe him to be dead. In fact, as Homer immediately lets us know, Odysseus is being held captive (for the purposes of sex, believe it or not) on the island of the goddess Kalypso. To make matters worse, Poseidon, the god of the sea, is ticked off at Odysseus, and sees no reason to let him get home.

Back in Ithaka, Odysseus's wife Penelope is getting swarmed by a horde of unwanted suitors. Odysseus and Penelope's son, Telemachos, now a teenager, gets visited by the goddess Athene (who was always chummy with Odysseus). She tells him to go in search of news of his missing father. He takes her advice, first traveling to Pylos to visit King Nestor. Nestor takes him in, feeds him well – and then tells him to go see King Menelaos in Sparta. Once again, he does as he's told.

In Sparta, Telemachos learns from Menelaos that Odysseus is alive and...well, being held captive on Kalypso's island. Menelaos also tells Telemachos about how his brother, King Agamemnon, was killed upon his return home from Troy by his unfaithful wife, Klytaimestra, and her lover, Aigisthos. Agamemnon was avenged by his son Orestes, who killed the murderers in return for their treachery. This isn't important to the plotline as much as it is a thematic point – it raises the question of whether Odysseus will be killed when he gets home, and, if so, whether Telemachos will step up to avenge his father's death. Meanwhile, back in Ithaka, Penelope's suitors plot to ambush and kill Telemachos when he returns home. Oh, the tension!

Up on Mount Olympos, where the gods all hang out, the goddess Athene asks her father, Zeus, the King of the gods, to have mercy on Odysseus and force Kalpyso to release him. Zeus says, "Whatever," and in no time, Odysseus sails off on a makeshift raft. Unfortunately, Poseidon whips up some storms, and instead of getting home, Odysseus washes ashore in the land of the Phaiakians. Fortunately, Athene makes the resident princess, Nausikaa, develop a crush on him. Nausikaa takes him home to meet her parents, the King and Queen of Phaiakia. In return for their hospitality, Odysseus tells them everything that's happened to him since the end of the Trojan War:

Odysseus left Troy with a ship of his Ithakan men. At their first stop, they plundered the locals' stuff. Several storm-tossed days later, they landed on the island of the Lotus-eaters. A few guys ate the lotus flower and forgot their homes and families, and had to be taken back to the ship by force.

Next, Odysseus and his men came to the land of the Cyclopses – giant one-eyed monsters. Odysseus and his men stumbled into a cave, which, unfortunately, belonged to one of these man-eating creatures. The Cyclops sealed the entrance to the cave with a huge boulder and ate a few of the Ithakans. Odysseus kept his cool, though, and told the monster his name was "Nobody." Then he got the Cyclops drunk on wine and stabbed it in the eye with a sharpened log. When the creature – whose name turns out to be Polyphemos – cried out that "Nobody is killing me," the other Cyclopses were like, "Then pipe down, already!" Odysseus is one clever dude.

Next, Odysseus tied his men under the bellies of Polyphemos's flock of sheep. The next morning, when the blinded monster opened the cave to let them out to pasture, he only touched the tops of the sheep to make sure nobody was riding them – and was duped again. The actual "Nobody" made his escape last, clinging to a ram. (Here's a picture of his escape.) The problem is, as Odysseus was sailing away with his men, his ego got the better of him. He taunted the Cyclops, telling him his real name. This was a dumb idea because Polyphemos was the son of Poseidon, the god of the sea. He prayed to his father to make Odysseus suffer. And suffer. And lose all his men. And maybe die too. This is why Poseidon hates our hero so much.

Next, Odysseus and his men came to the island of Aiolos, god of the wind. He helped Odysseus out by putting all the winds – except for the west-bound breeze they needed – into a nice little bag. Unfortunately, Odysseus didn't tell his men what's in the bag. On the way home, they opened it up, thinking it was full of treasure. Big mistake. All the winds jumped out and ran riot, thus driving them to the island of Circe, a sorceress. She turned many of the men into pigs. With the help of the gods, Odysseus got his men turned back into humans and had sex with Circe. For a year. Then one of his men said, "Can we get going already?" and Odysseus said, "OK." But then Circe instructed them that they had to go the Underworld and get advice from the prophet Teiresias. So off they went.

Teiresias prophesied that Odysseus would make it home, but not without difficulty. Odysseus spoke to several other famous dead people (like his war buddies Achilleus and Agamemnon). He also met the ghost of his mother, Antikleia, who had died of grief over her son's prolonged absence. Then, after a quick pit stop back at Circe's island, where they got some more

directions, Odysseus and his men sailed on.

Soon, they passed by the Sirens, monstrous women with beautiful voices who try to lure sailors to their deaths. Odysseus made his men plug their ears and tie him to the mast so he could listen to the song without chasing after it. In this way, he became the only man to hear the Sirens' song and survive.

Next they met two horrible monsters, also female, named Skylla and Charybdis. As predicted by Circe, Skylla (who has six heads) ate six Ithakans; the rest barely escaped Charybdis (a giant vortex who sucks up the sea and vomits it back out again). After that they landed on the island of Helios, the sun god, where his very special cattle were kept. Despite having been warned by Teiresias and Circe not to eat the cattle, Odysseus's men couldn't control their hunger. Bad call. Not long afterward, everyone died in a storm – except for Odysseus. He wound up on Kalypso's island, where he was held prisoner for seven years.

So, that's it for Odysseus's story to the Phaiakians. They are so moved by his suffering that they load him up with treasure and ferry him back to Ithaka. (Unfortunately, in return for their trouble, the god Poseidon turns them and their ship into stone.) Once Odysseus gets home, Athene disguises him as a beggar so he can scope out the situation. Odysseus then recruits the assistance of the swineherd, Eumaios, who puts him up for the night while Athene flies to Sparta to retrieve Telemachos. When Telemachos gets back, Odysseus reveals himself to his son. Then Odysseus heads to the palace, still disguised as a beggar. Without revealing his true identity, he talks to Penelope and tries to convince her that Odysseus is on his way home. She doesn't believe him. Odysseus uses this opportunity to see which of his servants are still loyal to the household and which have joined the suitors.

At a certain point, Penelope, tired of waiting around, offers the suitors a test: she sets up a contest of physical prowess and declares that she will marry the winner. The deal is, all the men have to try to string Odysseus's old bow and shoot it through the heads of twelve axes. Many suitors try and fail – until the beggar (Odysseus in disguise) asks for a chance to try. He succeeds, drops the disguise, and, with the help of Telemachos, several loyal servants, and Athene's protection, kills all the suitors in a massive and bloody slaughter. Then Odysseus reunites with his wife, and everything seems hunky-dory – except for the detail that he's just killed all the young noblemen of Ithaka and their parents are furious.

The next morning, Odysseus leaves the palace, reunites with his father Laertes, and lays low while the angry moms and dads start looking for vengeance. Just when it looks like more violence is on the way, Athene appears and tells everyone to just quit it already: let's all settle down and get along. This sounds like a good idea to everyone, and peace is restored in Ithaka.

Book I

- The poet invokes the Muse to help him tell the story of Odysseus. How original.
- We learn that Poseidon, god of the sea, holds a grudge (though we don't know exactly why) against Odysseus and makes the mortal's seaward journey difficult. This tells us two

very important things: one, Greek gods are temperamental, and two, Poseidon is a powerful guy.

- So Poseidon isn't around on Mount Olympos (presumably because he's busy getting sweet revenge) while the other gods discuss the fact that this one guy Orestes murdered this other guy Aigisthos.
- Zeus, king of the gods and player-extraordinaire, says that Aigisthos deserved death because he had a long affair with Agamemnon's wife while he was away at Troy and then killed Agamemnon upon returning home.
- Turns out Aigisthos had been warned by Hermes (the messenger of the gods) not to do this. In fact, Hermes pretty much explicitly said, "If you touch this guy's wife and then kill him, then Orestes is going to pop a cap in you." And still Aigisthos ignored the advice.
- Additionally, because Orestes is Agamemnon's son, he was only avenging his father by killing Aigisthos. Yes, we would consider this murder, but the Greeks were pretty serious about the whole avenging-the-father thing. Let's just call it "justifiable homicide" in the eyes of the gods.
- Athene, who clearly doesn't give a crab's apple about Orestes, decides Zeus should be thinking less about him and more about her all time favorite mortal, Odysseus. So she asks for Zeus (who is *her* father, by the way) to have mercy on her favorite captain (who has been trying to get home now for something around twenty years).
- Zeus claims that he has not forgotten Odysseus's plight, though we all know he's just making excuses.
- Zeus reveals a little more of the Poseidon grudge story: the god is angry at Odysseus because the mortal poked out the eye of Polyphemos, Poseidon's son.
- Still, Poseidon isn't out to kill Odysseus, just make his life a living hell by hindering his journey home.
- Zeus comments that Poseidon will need to stop pouting at some point and get over himself already, since all the other gods like Odysseus so much.
- We learn that Odysseus at this very moment is being held captive by a nymph named Kalypso.
- Athene wants to send the gods' messenger Hermes to go tell Kalypso that she really needs to let Odysseus go (you know, so he can get back to his wife and child and all).
- Zeus, to remind everyone that HE'S THE BOSS, decides not to send Hermes. Yet.
- Athene, reminding everyone that in fact, she's the boss, goes to Ithaka disguised as Mentes, a family friend of Odysseus's and the ruler of the Taphians. Oh, and also a man.
- Which brings us to Ithaka, where a bevy of suitors is milling about (for reasons which will be soon disclosed).
- Once Mentes/Athene arrives, these suitors do what they do best, namely lounge around lazily. Odysseus's son Telemachos, very clearly neither lazy nor a suitor, gets up hastily to welcome his guest. He even prepares a banquet in Mentes's honor.
- Historical Context Note: Hospitality was a big deal in the ancient world. When guests showed up, they were expected to be good guests (bring gifts and behave themselves). Likewise, the hosts were expected to, well, be good hosts (provide food and shelter). Just keep in mind that breaking these rules was a huge social taboo.
- So Telemachos apologizes to Mentes for the suitors' rudeness, hints that it would be different if his father were here, and asks who this guest is.
- The point is, Telemachos didn't know this guest was Mentes (or Athene), yet he still pulled out all the stops to play the good host.

- Athene responds as Mentes and advises the boy to not give up hope of his father Odysseus coming home.
- She asks about the suitors and Telemachos replies that he cannot make them go away; he wishes Odysseus were here to fend them off.
- Why, you ask? Well, we learn that the suitors are selfishly eating all of the household's food and giving nothing in return while hoping Odysseus's wife Penelope will marry one of them before her husband gets back into town.
- (Actually, Odysseus has taken so long coming back from the Trojan war they're all convinced he's dead. Also, Penelope is super-attractive, which explains why everyone wants to marry her.)
- This is an example of breaking the guest-host bond of good behavior.
- So Athene advises Telemachos to go to Pylos and talk to Nestor, and then head to Sparta to see King Menelaos, who has red hair, which is apparently an important feature to mention.
- And when he's done with this, he should think about how to kill all these suitors, because by then it will probably be about time for some sweet revenge.
- As Mentes leaves, Telemachos tries to offer him gifts, as well as a bath and bed for the night, but Mentes politely declines.
- After she leaves, Athene fills Telemachos with a vision of his father so he can realize he was in the presence of a divine spirit. But he still doesn't know it was Athene.
- Now it's about time for some music, so Phemios the bard sings about the Trojan War.
- This is rather an insensitive choice of subject matter, since the elephant in the room is that Odysseus's absence is probably the result of his dying...in the Trojan War.
- Penelope, who obviously agrees with our "insensitive" label, comes down from her room to politely request that he sing another song, preferably not one about her most likely dead husband.
- Telemachos reproaches his mother and allows Phemios to keep singing.
- Actually, Telemachos quite rationally explains that it's not the poet's fault Odysseus hasn't come home. Obviously it's Zeus's fault. Besides, lots of other families lost their men in the war, and you don't see them running around crying their heads off.
- Penelope is struck by Telemachos's wisdom (callousness?) and goes back upstairs to sleep.
- Telemachos, all piss and vinegar and still high with courage from his visit with the divine, tells the suitors that they must leave at dawn. So there!
- Antinoös, one of the suitors, protests. He claims that Ithaka needs a king and that the suitors are here to provide one.
- Eurymachos, another suitor, asks who the stranger was and if he brought any news of Odysseus.
- Telemachos lies; he says he's heard the news that Odysseus is dead. Then he reveals that the visitor was Mentes (although he himself knows there was some divine power involved).
- Telemachos goes up to bed where the nurse Eurykleia, who was the servant of Laertes, Odysseus's father, takes care of him.
- He falls asleep considering Athene's advice.

Book II

- Telemachos calls a meeting of all the Ithakan men. The suitors come too.
- Lord Aigyptios (not to be confused with Aigisthos, the man whose murder the gods were earlier discussing), want to know why. After all, there haven't been any meetings since Odysseus left.
- Considering it's been almost twenty years, we're thinking these Ithakans aren't exactly bureaucratic go-getters.
- Telemachos grouses for a bit about the shameful actions of the suitors who have invaded his house, eaten his food, and drank his wine. Oh, and spent all their time devising ways to try and get with his mother (p.s. she's not interested).
- Nobody dares challenge his righteous anger except Antinoös, the would-be-king we met earlier. He blames Penelope herself for deceiving the suitors.
- How so? Well, he explains:
- When Odysseus went missing instead of coming home from the Trojan War, Penelope devised a plan to delay having to marry one of these suitors.
- (Note: Because she was a Queen, Penelope would have been expected to marry after her husband died. Part of her duty to her land is making sure that her people have a king.)
- So to stall, she said she would weave a funeral shroud for Laertes, Odysseus's father. By day, she wove. By night, while everyone was sleeping and none-too-watchful, she unraveled all her day's work.
- Magically, it appeared the shroud would never be done!
- Of course, no one ever figured her out. Until a maid blabbed on her.
- (Even more amazing, however, is the fact that Penelope is weaving a funeral shroud for a man who isn't dead; Odysseus's father is elderly but hanging on.)
- Finished with his Penelope story, Antinoös issues an ultimatum; he commands that Telemachos either get rid of Penelope (we're not exactly sure how that would work) or make her choose a suitor for a husband.
- Telemachos refuses to oust his mother from the house.
- He is likely on the verge of refusing the *second* option when Zeus intervenes by sending a sign from above; two eagles fly down from a mountain and attack the people of the city.
- Halitherses, an augur whose job it is to read portentous signs, reads the portentous sign. He decides it is an omen that Odysseus will return home.
- (Don't ask us how he knew that.)
- Eurymachos, another suitor, laughs at the old augur and declares that Odysseus is dead. He tells Telemachos that the suitors fear neither him nor his diviners with their talk of signs.
- Bad move, man.
- Telemachos is done arguing. He tells the men he is sailing for Pylos to hear news of his father.
- Mentor, an old friend of Odysseus's, speaks up. (Yes, his name really is Mentor. Actually, we only have the word "mentor" in our language because it's this guy's name. Seriously.)
- Anyway, Mentor announces how sickening it is that the community at large has not risen to speak against the suitors. Yes – surely all will be incited to action!
- Sadly, no. Another townsman quickly hushes Mentor, so the crowd does nothing.
- Foiled again!
- The meeting is over.

- Telemachos prays to the god who visited him last night, whoever it was.
- Athene, nearby, hears his prayer and descends in the guise of Mentor. He/she tells Telemachos to prepare provisions for the journey and promises to find a ship for him to take.
- When Telemachos goes home, the suitors mock him.
- Telemachos ignores them.
- In confidence, he tells Eurykleia to prepare food and wine with which to sail and to keep this whole trip on the down-low – especially from Penelope. Eurykleia agrees.
- Athene, to mix things up a bit, disguises herself as Telemachos while roaming about town and gathering up some good-hearted men to come along as crew for the ship.
- Speaking of, she also needs a ship, which she gets from Noëmon (a wealthy ship-seller – looks like you could pick these things up at the corner store back in the day). She then approaches Telemachos (still disguised as Mentor) with news that his ride is ready.
- Telemachos leaves immediately, taking with him a group of trusted men and of course Athene/Mentor as well, who is a very convenient travel companion.

Book III

- At dawn the next day, Telemachos arrives in Pylos to find the citizens making sacrifices to Poseidon. They tend to do that a lot, and it's probably not unrelated to the two key facts we discussed earlier, that Poseidon is both powerful and highly temperamental.
- Telemachos is nervous about having to deliver a speech (which you had to do whenever you arrived anywhere, it seems) in front of nobility like Nestor, but Mentor/Athene encourages him: she tells him to have faith in himself because the gods favor him.
- This is a good thing to hear – especially in ancient Greece.
- Still, before any speeches are made, the Ithakans are invited to a sacrificial feast.
- Peisistratos, a son of Nestor, gives wine to Mentor/Athene and asks him to make a prayer to Poseidon.
- Mentor/Athene prays to Poseidon to honor Nestor and his sons and his kingdom and then fulfills the request for honor herself – because she's a goddess.
- After they feast, Nestor asks the Ithakans where they came from and what their business here is.
- Telemachos, all jazzed up for his big speech, introduces them and asks for news about Odysseus (whom Nestor fought alongside at Troy).
- Nestor, reminded of the Trojan War, laments how long and difficult it was.
- Then he speaks kindly of Odysseus and remarks on how much Telemachos is like his dad.
- And then it's more story time. Nestor details that, after their success at Troy, the Greeks had some trouble (obviously the fault of the gods) returning home. Athene, in particular, made it difficult for them. (See?)
- Menelaos and Agamemnon, two brothers and also two Greek kings, argued as brothers (and kings) tend to do. Menelaos decided to take his fleet and leave Troy immediately while Agamemnon stayed behind, making sacrifices to try and appease Athene.
- The army, unable to reach a unanimous decision on which man to follow, splits up. Those armies, always needing someone else to tell them what to do.

- Odysseus decided to side with Menelaos and so took his ships to sea.
- Except then he changed his mind.
- On returning to Troy to show loyalty to Agamemnon, he took half of Menelaos's ships with him. Menelaos and the remainder of the ships, including Nestor, safely made their way home.
- Agamemnon, as everyone knows, came home only to be killed by his scheming wife Klytaimestra and her lover Aigisthos. (This is the murder the gods were discussing at the very beginning of the poem.)
- Telemachos says he envies Orestes for taking sweet revenge and wishes the gods would help him avenge himself similarly on the suitors.
- Nestor reminds him that Odysseus was a great favorite of Athene and that there is hope yet that he might come home.
- Telemachos humbly disagrees – he thinks it's wishful thinking to believe the gods are on his side.
- Mentor/Athene interrupts; she claims Telemachos underestimates the gods. After all, they can save a man simply by the power of their will.
- Telemachos asks Nestor for more details about Agamemnon's death.
- Nestor tells the story:
- Klytaimestra, Agamemnon's wife, has an affair with Aigisthos while her husband's away. While all this adultery is going on, Agamemnon's brother Menelaos is stranded in Egypt, which is why there was no vengeance being exacted on behalf of the absent king.
- Agamemnon comes home and is promptly killed by his treacherous wife and her equally treacherous lover.
- The treacherous pair reigns for seven years in Agamemnon's (former) kingdom of Mykene.
- In the eighth year, Orestes, Agamemnon's son, comes "back from exile" and kills Klytaimestra and Aigisthos.
- On the funeral day of the treacherous couple, Menelaos finally arrives home. He's quite sad to find his brother is dead.
- The end.
- Having finished his story, Nestor warns Telemachos not to stay away from home too long, since the suitors are hanging out unchaperoned back there.
- But then, he urges the young man to go to Sparta and see King Menelaos, who has just returned home himself, and ask him for news of Odysseus.
- Mentor/Athene tells them to make their ritual sacrifice to Poseidon and go to sleep.
- As Telemachos and Mentor/Athene are heading back towards the ships, Nestor offers them all beds for the night. More of that good Greek hospitality.
- Telemachos accepts, and Athene finally reveals herself by turning into an eagle. She decides to stay and watch over Telemachos's crew while he burns rubber to Sparta.
- Nestor is awed that she is helping Telemachos and promises to make a sacrifice of a golden-horned heifer to her. Yes! The gods love their cows.
- At dawn, Nestor arrives with his sons and makes good on his word.
- They perform a sacrifice (yes, another one) and Nestor invites Telemachos's whole crew to the following feast.
- Afterwards, he provides Telemachos horses so he can go to Sparta. Nestor's son Peisistratos accompanies him (*someone* had to keep an eye on those horses).
- Two days of fun chariot-traveling follow.

Book IV

- When Telemachos arrives, Menelaos is hosting a double wedding feast.
- Telemachos is welcomed into the palace and totally awed by the place.
- Menelaos serves them food before asking them to speak, which is a nice thing to do.
- During the feast, Telemachos cannot help but whisper to Menelaos his wonder at the incredible palace.
- Menelaos agrees; he was pretty happy to see it again after wandering the seas for seven years. But he quickly moves on from this happy note to tell of his sorrow at discovering his brother Agamemnon murdered.
- Also, he lost a lot of friends in the Trojan war.
- Menelaos misses Odysseus more than anyone, he says (although we think Penelope is probably a good contender for that title).
- It's during this remark that Menelaos finally recognizes Telemachos as Odysseus's son. (Remember, he insisted on feasting with the newly arrived guests before hearing any tale of who they were or what they came for.)
- Telemachos, meanwhile, has broken down at hearing the King talk so fondly about his father. He cries. Awkward silence.
- Helen, Menelaos's wife (and yes, the woman that started the whole Trojan war to begin with by getting herself stolen) enters and breaks the silence tactfully; she remarks on how much Telemachos resembles Odysseus.
- This breaks the tension and Menelaos fondly recognizes Peisistratos as Nestor's son as well.
- Everyone gets back to eating.
- Helen decides to drug the men's wine with an anodyne of forgetfulness, hoping to soothe away their sorrows.
- After treating the wine, she serves it and tells funny stories about Odysseus.
- Helen tells about a time when Odysseus disguised himself as Trojan beggar – even beating himself up to make it look convincing – to get information from the Trojans. Ah, that was a good one.
- Then Menelaos recounts the time they were inside the Trojan horse and Helen, whose loyalty apparently lay with the Trojans at the time, came around knocking on the horse and calling each man inside in the voice of his wife. Odysseus saved everyone from giving themselves away by urging them into silence and even clapping his hands over one man's mouth.
- Everyone enjoys these stories, clearly, and they're all too drugged by the wine to feel any sadness. Telemachos suggests they all go to sleep.
- In the morning, Menelaos finally asks Telemachos why he has come.
- Telemachos explains his situation and asks for news of his father.
- Menelaos is angry that suitors are annoying Odysseus's household. He tells Telemachos another story.
- Once, when Menelaos was stranded on the island of Pharos, Eidothea, one of the resident nymphs, advised him to capture the god of the island – Proteus – and hold him captive.
- Normally, this would be suicidal, and therefore a really bad idea, but in this case, it's the

only way the god will tell them how to get off the island.

- Eidothea helps disguise Menelaos and three of his men as seals. When Proteus surfaces to count his seal flock, they pounce on him and cling desperately while he shape-shifts into several different beings.
- Finally, either because he gives up or because they were willing to cling to that much garbage, Proteus decides to answer their questions.
- He reveals that Menelaos is trapped at Pharos because he didn't offer a proper sacrifice to Zeus before departing.
- The only way he can appease the now-angry god is by going to the Nile River and making them an offering.
- With the diagnosis out of the way, Menelaos asks Proteus for news of his Greek friends.
- Proteus tells him that Aias (little Aias that is) has died for foolishly challenging the gods.
- [Mythological Context Lesson: Don't get confused; there are two different characters named Aias in Greek mythology and they are of no blood-relation to each other. You may have heard of their names as Ajax, the Latin version of his name, which became the standard English version, for some reason. This one here is called little Aias, and the other is called big Aias, or, just as often, Telamonian Aias (his dad was a dude name Telamon). The deal with little Aias is that he raped and killed Kassandra (a Trojan Princess) on the altar of Athene. This was a big no-no—both for obvious reasons and because altars were sacred spaces. For his offense he was killed by the gods, so this references yet another lesson in piety.]
- Menelaos adds that Agamemnon is dead (which we've now been told numerous times).
- Lastly, we come to Odysseus. Proteus reveals that the man is being held as a prisoner of Kalypso and longs to go home.
- Menelaos is all, "Thanks, man" and gets off the island.
- OK so that's it for Menelaos's story.
- He wants Telemachos to stay with him longer, but Telemachos begs leave because his men are back at Pylos with Nestor.
- When Menelaos offers him practical gifts of horses and a chariot, Telemachos refuses them and asks instead for a keepsake.
- Menelaos gives him a silver bowl set.
- In the meantime, back at Ithaka, Noëmon, the rich merchant who sold Mentor/Athene the ship, asks Antinoös when Telemachos will be back from Pylos because he needs his ship. Athene appears to have not negotiated much longevity in the ship deal.
- Antinoös freaks out because he didn't know about Telemachos's voyage at all. (Or else he wasn't listening when Telemachos TOLD THEM ABOUT IT at the council meeting.) Mostly, he just gets all riled up because he's a jerk.
- So he calls a meeting with all the other suitors. Since Telemachos has been making their parasitic lifestyle so difficult and also, they all pretty much hate him, the men decide to sail out to sea, ambush the young man on his way home, and send him to his death.
- Medon, the town crier whose job it is to make public announcements, overhears this and makes a not-so-public announcement to Penelope, who freaks out. We think she's justified.
- She didn't know about the voyage either and laments wildly – first for her lost Odysseus, then for her son who is about to die.
- Eurykleia, the old nurse, feels guilty about concealing the journey from Penelope and begs her mistress to pray to Athene for Telemachos's sake.

- Penelope does, and Athene hears her. (She's got good ears, that goddess.)
- Meanwhile, down at the docks, the suitors have set sail.
- Athene, pitying Penelope, sends an image of the queen's sister – Iphthime – to her in her sleep. Iphthime assures her sister that Telemachos will come home safely. When Penelope doesn't believe her, the hallucinatory sister reveals that he has Athene's help.
- Penelope, all reassured by this, asks for news on Odysseus. Before answering, Iphthime fades away.
- Penelope wakes up feeling as fresh as a daisy.
- Meanwhile, the suitors wait in ambush.

Book V

- Athene implores her father Zeus to have mercy on Odysseus, who is trapped on Kalypso's island and sorely homesick.
- Zeus reassures her that Odysseus will be safe.
- But he does send the messenger Hermes to Kalypso's islands with instructions to let Odysseus go and, adding insult to injury, to help him build a sturdy escape raft.
- He then prophecies that Odysseus, after some trials at sea, will reach the island of Scheria alone, where the Phaiakians will befriend him and provide transport home.
- Hermes takes Zeus's message to Kalypso. Her island home is exotic and lovely, and we're guessing she is too, but after seven years Odysseus is blind to all. Instead, he roams the shore looking broken-heartedly out to sea.
- Kalypso, recognizing Hermes as a God, greets him with hospitality…
- …Until he delivers his news. Kalypso, afraid of losing Odysseus, gets quite spiteful. She accuses the gods of hating it when immortal women (like herself) lay with mortal men (like Odysseus).
- The elephant in the room, or rather, in Kalypso's speech, is that Zeus and other immortal men sleep with mortal women all the time, and no one ever gets upset over *that*.
- She points out that she rescued Odysseus before she decided to imprison him.
- Hermes does the wise thing and lets Kalypso run herself in circles griping until she gets exhausted and gives in. She grudgingly agrees to let Odysseus go and provision him for his journey.
- When Odysseus hears the news, he is suspicious of Kalypso's motives and won't accept her help until she vows not to work any more magic against him.
- She obeys, and everything's dandy between them again. No hard feelings. Really.
- Together, the couple builds a sound raft and supplies it with food and water. It takes them four days.
- On the fifth day Odysseus departs, having been given directions by Kalypso.
- Then trouble comes. Poseidon returns from hanging out at the end of the world and sees Odysseus roaming the open seas again.
- He is not pleased.
- So Poseidon draws up a storm which annihilates Odysseus's raft and almost drowns him.
- Odysseus despairs, wishing he could've died a glorious death at Troy rather than alone and dishonored at sea.

- Just in the nick of time, divine help arrives. The nereid (a.k.a. sea-nymph) Ino springs up and gives Odysseus some advice.
- Unfortunately, the advice is to abandon the raft and swim solo.
- To help Odysseus, Ino gives him her veil. If he wears it as a sash, it will keep him afloat and prevent him from drowning. Kind of like a life vest.
- Odysseus doubts her (not that you can blame him) and doesn't jump ship (raft?) after Ino leaves.
- But then a big wave crests over him (like a sign from above!) and he decides he'd better listen to the pretty lady.
- It's looking pretty bad for Odysseus, and Poseidon seems content to just let the storm do its thing.
- Athene very wisely waits for a self-satisfied Poseidon to leave before she arrives and calms the seas. She then sets up a wind to blow Odysseus toward land.
- This is what those English majors call a *deus ex machina*, when a god comes out of nowhere and helps like that. (Technically, the phrase means "a god out of the machine." This is because, in ancient theatrical performances, they would sometimes use a "machine"—basically an elevator operated by a pulley—to have a god descend from the "heavens." Whoa… special effects! Of course, if you want to get REALLY technical, since Athene is the one doing the appearing here, this is a *dea ex machine*: "a goddess out of the machine.")
- Odysseus floats for two days at sea, presumably getting blown via Athene's devices before spotting land.
- Unfortunately, it is some very rocky land and Odysseus is afraid he might cut himself on the jagged edges, so he holds out for smoother shores.
- Athene guides him to the mouth of a stream, since streams make for cushy landings.
- Odysseus prays to the river god to let him rest there and is accordingly granted safe passage.
- As he climbs ashore, he complains about how much he suffered.
- He's still complaining. OK he's done. But only because Athene eases his mind and helps him find some thick bushes under which he digs and falls asleep exhausted in a bed of leaves. Nice and cozy.

Book VI

- As he sleeps, Athene enters the city where Odysseus has crash-landed and heads to the bedroom of the beautiful princess Nausikaa.
- Taking the form of the princess's friend, the goddess enters Nausikaa's dream and explains that, while the single life is in fact nice, it's time for her to think about marriage. She urges the princess to go to the streams and wash her wedding linens.
- When she awakes, young Nausikaa asks her father for the gig (as in, a mule-cart) to take her laundry to the streams. But she doesn't mention anything about marriage to him.
- When her party gets to the streams, they wash their clothes and play around on the shore.
- Nausikaa is so beautiful that she looks like the goddess Artemis (yet another Greek virgin).
- The girls' shouting wakes Odysseus and he rises, naked (!), to see who it is. He covers

himself with an olive branch.

- Everyone scatters at the sight of the big, scary, nearly-naked man. Everyone except Nausikaa, who stays because Athene gives her courage.
- Odysseus considers whether he should fall and hug her knees or use his eloquent speech to convince her that he needs some help.
- Predictably, cunning Odysseus chooses the latter, demonstrating how civilized he is. He praises her beauty, tells her his situation, and effectively begs for her aid.
- Nausikaa is touched by his story and wants to be of service. She calls her maids out of hiding to help him bathe. (What?)
- Odysseus, always the gentleman, begs to bathe alone – he doesn't want to offend the young girls by letting them see him naked.
- When he's done, he puts on some clothes that the princess gave him and Athene plays up his good looks. Nausikaa is struck with wonder. She tells her maids that she wants a man who looks like Odysseus for a husband.
- Uh-oh.
- The princess gives Odysseus some instructions, that will get him back to the palace to meet the rest of the Phaiakians.
- Wait a minute… Phaiakians…on the island of Scheria…this sounds familiar…oh, right, Zeus and that prediction.
- She rambles on a bit about her people, who are apparently terrible archers and great at building ships, a particularly juicy tidbit for a stranded man with no possessions who's trying to sail back home to his family.
- Once she's done dropping unintentional hints, the princess tells Odysseus to follow her train of accompanying servant-folk into town and ignore the crude remarks of the seamen they will pass on the way.
- Once they get to town, she says, he should hang out in the garden while she goes inside.
- Then, when the time is right, he should come inside, find her mother the Queen, and hug her knees while he begs for mercy.
- Apparently everything depends on the Queen's opinion. If he can get her on his side, he's all set for hospitality and help in this country.
- Now that Nausikaa has laid out the plans, everyone follows them.
- While Odysseus waits in the gardens, he prays to Athene for luck.
- Athene hears him.

Book VII

- Nausikaa arrives at home.
- Meanwhile, Athene disguises Odysseus in a cloud of sea mist so nobody can see him as he wanders the city. Cool beans. Also cool, Virgil took this concept and used it in the *Aeneid*.
- Because she is a fan of pretending to be other people, Athene comes to Odysseus in the form of a child.
- Odysseus asks the adorable little girl for directions to the palace, and she leads him there.
- Along the way, she tells him all about the land and the ruling family. (This is a very

informed child. Think Hermione but immortal and in disguise.)

- So here's the 411: the Queen's name is Arete and the King's Alkinoös (not to be confused with the icky suitor Antinoös).
- Also, we are reminded that the Queen is calling the shots, so she's the one to talk up once Odysseus gets to the palace, which is apparently just as stunning as Menelaos's palace that we saw back in Book IV.
- Athene/the suspiciously knowledgeable little girl takes Odysseus directly to Queen Arete. Odysseus, who is really good at following directions, falls and hugs her knees.
- At that moment, his protective mist cloud disappears and everyone sees him.
- Stunned silence.
- Odysseus makes his plea.
- More stunned silence.
- Then, the King's oracle nervously clears his throat. All eyes turn to him, and he scolds the King for not showing this beggar some hospitality.
- This breaks the ice and everyone rushes to serve Odysseus. Alkinoös even makes one of the princes give up his seat for Odysseus.
- The King orders that the morrow will be made a festal day in honor of this guest. That is quite a welcome for an oddly-clothed stranger.
- Actually, this is another great example of that good ancient hospitality.
- After much eating and fuss, Alkinoös gets around to asking of Odysseus the question that's on everyone's mind: "Hey, any chance you're a god?"
- Odysseus assures everyone that no, he isn't and then asks for the Phaiakians to build him a ship so he can go home.
- Everyone is all, "Sure!"
- The Queen, however, is busy looking at Odysseus's clothes, which appear suspiciously similar to the ones she had made for her daughter Nausikaa.
- So she asks Odysseus as politely as one can ask, "What the heck are you doing wearing my daughter's clothes!?"
- Odysseus realizes he had better choose his words carefully, as his story had better not include the virginal princess taking off her clothes at any point. So he says something along the lines of, "Well, that's a long story."
- Except that isn't going to cut it, so he launches into the quick and dirty, starting with Kalypso and ending with Nausikaa, without revealing who he is.
- Everyone is moved by his words.
- They're all touched by his story and grow sympathetic.
- King Alkinoös was apparently very touched, as he offers up Nausikaa's hand in marriage.
- Then again, he says, if Odysseus doesn't want to marry the princess, the King will make sure his men row him wherever he wants to go.
- Odysseus decides to go home.
- Bed time for all.

Book VIII

- At dawn, Athene takes on the disguise of the town crier and goes around the city shouting

the news of the stranger's coming and the upcoming feast. Everyone congregates, curious, at the palace.

- She also makes Odysseus totally studly in their eyes and instills in him a desire to prove himself worthy of any challenge.
- At this little meeting, Alkinoös orders that a ship and crew be prepared for later that day.
- The King then invites everyone to the banquet and calls in his bard, Demodokos, who is a great singer but blind.
- (Oh, p.s., it's likely that Homer himself was blind.)
- Demodokos sings the story of the fight between Odysseus and Achilleus (whom you know as Achilles) that went down before the Trojan War.
- Odysseus, his name still unknown to the Phaiakians, sits back to listen to the tale about…himself. It brings tears to his eyes. He hides his face beneath his cloak and only King Alkinoös notices his tears.
- Alkinoös orders some sporting games.
- The King brags to Odysseus that when he goes home, he will boast to his people of the Phaiakians' athleticism.
- They play. Homer lists the names of all the men that partake and the winners of each race.
- You should note that the King's sons make a good showing; Prince Klytoneos wins the foot-race and Prince Laodamas wins the boxing match.
- It is this very Prince Laodamas, a handsome man, by the way, who invites Odysseus to join in the games.
- When he proves reluctant, Euryalos (another competitor) jokingly says he doesn't look like the athletic type.
- This is literary foreshadowing for Odysesseus kicking some serious butt.
- Odysseus proceeds to hurl a discus further than any man present has managed so far. (Athene, disguised as a Phaiakian, is the one to measure the distance and announce as much.)
- Odysseus proudly asks for any man to challenge him. He will take on anyone, he says, except his gracious host, Prince Laodamas.
- He thinks he can win any contest except the running race since his long days at sea have weakened his legs.
- Alkinoös wisely decides to diffuse the situation by switching things up; he asks for Demodokos to come back and sing some more.
- Demodokos is led in and sings the story of the affair between Ares (god of war) and Aphrodite (goddess of love), and of how Hephaistos, Aphrodite's crippled blacksmith husband, got jealous when he found out. The scorned husband wove a net, spread it over the bed, caught the lovers in the act, and shamed them in front of all the other gods.
- Well, apparently that was enough storytelling for the King. Alkinoös orders some dancing to entertain Odysseus and bestows on his guest a few gifts.
- Euryalos approaches Odysseus and offers him a lovely sword in repentance for his rash words earlier. Odysseus forgives him.
- Later, after being given a nice bath, Odysseus makes a request of Demodokos to sing of that great man Odysseus in the Trojan horse.
- Demodokos complies and his song makes Odysseus cry, which he again tries to hide behind his cloak.
- Alkinoös sees and begs Demodokos to stop since it is upsetting his guest.
- Finally, Alkinoös asks who his guest is and why he grieves so much when hearing about

the Trojan War. He silences his bard and invites him to tell his tale, but not before a complete non sequitur in which he tells everyone of a prophecy that one of his ships will be turned to stone and mountains thrown up around his city.

- Everyone is all, "Um…OK" and then gets ready to hear Odysseus's story.
- Take a deep breath, folks. This is going to be a long tale.

Book IX

- Odysseus introduces himself and begins to tell his story, starting with the moment his men leave Troy. We've got almost ten years to cover here.
- He starts by describing his home – the island of Ithaka of course – and all of the surrounding islands.
- He laments that he was held captive by Kalypso, and actually declares (in our Lattimore translation) that she "never could […] persuade the heart within me" to be her lover. (Basically, he means that he was acting like he loved her, but didn't feel that way in his heart.)
- Now Odysseus covers the stuff we don't know – the years in between Troy and Kalypso. Also, welcome to the historical present.
- Odysseus and his men first come to the land of the Kikonians, where they kill everyone, take plunder, and enslave the women.
- Odysseus tries to get his men to go back to sea so they can get home already, but the men are starving and therefore mutinous. Many Ithakans are killed in the plundering struggle (the natives put up a fight).
- Those who escape are victims of a god-sent storm and have to wait around for a few days before they can sail again.
- Ten days later, they land on the island of the Lotus Eaters.
- This sounds like a great tropical get-away, which is exciting until three of Odysseus's men eat the lotus flower, lose their memory of home and family, and want nothing more than to stay on the island…forever.
- Odysseus quickly rounds up his men, including the three lotus-afflicted guys, and leaves.
- Next they arrive at the land of the uncivilized Cyclopes, giant monsters with only one eye. Because of their uncivilized ways, these monsters have no seamanship and let their fertile land go to waste. All they do is tend flocks of sheep.
- When Odysseus and his crew run across a Cyclops's deserted cave, his men want to steal from there – but Odysseus won't let them.
- Instead, he wants to treat the Cyclops like a human being and play the part of good guests (more on that hospitality thing). So they burn an offering in the monster's cave and wait for his return.
- Not surprisingly, the Cyclops soon returns, driving in his herd of sheep and closing the entrance of the cave behind him with a huge boulder.
- Then he's all, "What are you doing in my cave?"
- After some bantering he refuses their suggestion of hospitality – he doesn't care for Zeus's rules about being good guests and hosts.
- The Cyclops asks Odysseus where he has landed his ship. Odysseus, quick on his feet,

says that they have been shipwrecked by Poseidon (this will make for some gorgeous irony in a few pages).

- The Cyclops, also quick on his feet, bends down, grabs two men, and promptly eats them.
- Then he goes to sleep.
- Odysseus draws his sword, meaning to kill the Cyclops in his sleep. But he stops when he realizes that they can never escape the cave without the strength of the Cyclops to remove the gigantic rock at the entrance. Foiled again.
- So they mill around and wait for the monster to wake up and have breakfast.
- The Cyclops wakes in the morning and, yes, has a few of Odysseus's men for breakfast.
- When he leaves to tend his flocks for the day, Odysseus hatches and plots a plan. He has his men carve out a huge wooden pole and sharpen its end in fire.
- When the Cyclops returns, Odysseus cunningly offers him wine and tells him that his name is "Nobody."
- The Cyclops gets drunk from the wine and passes out.
- Time for action. Odysseus and his men drive the sharpened pole straight into the Cyclops's only eye, blinding him.
- The Cyclops makes such a racket in his pain that other Cyclopes gather outside his cave and ask him what is wrong. We hear his name – Polyphemos – for the first time. They ask if any man has tricked him.
- Polyphemos yells out to them: "Nobody's tricked me, Nobody's ruined me!"
- So the others are all, "OK, fine, then stop making a ruckus. Nobody's ruined us, either" and they go back to their fun times in the pastures.
- But first, they reveal the information that Poseidon, god of the sea, is Polyphemos's father.
- Uh-oh.
- Odysseus takes a moment to congratulate himself.
- But there still in the little problem of how to escape the cave. The Cyclops, meanwhile, can't see anything and therefore can't grab up the men to eat them for their treachery, so he just gives up and goes to bed after pulling the spike out of his eye.
- While he sleeps, Odysseus devises yet another plan: he ties each of his men beneath one of Polyphemos's rams, saving the biggest for himself, of course.
- The next morning, Polyphemos lets his flock out, reaching down and feeling the tops of their fleece for escaping men. Of course, he doesn't detect anything.
- Odysseus's ram is the last one out and Polyphemos asks him (the ram) what is wrong; he is usually the first out. He decides that his king ram must be sympathizing with his master because of the whole mutilated eye thing and lets the creature pass.
- Outside, Odysseus triumphantly unties his men and all make their way to their ship, stealing the escape-vessel sheep while they're at it.
- Sweet – surely they are home-free?
- Nope. Odysseus cannot help taunting Polyphemos as they sail away. We're sensing a trend here.
- Polyphemos, enraged, throws a gigantic rock that passes over the Ithakans' ship.
- The men are frightened and rather reasonably want Odysseus to stop taunting Polyphemos, but he's having too much fun trash-talking.
- He then pulls the moronic move of revealing his real name to Polyphemos. In fact, he doesn't just reveal his name; he basically delivers his personal biography: he is Odysseus, raider of cities, Laertes's son, the man from Ithaka.
- Polyphemos, quite a tattle-tale, runs to Poseidon and prays that he curse Odysseus. He

wishes that Odysseus will never get home, or if he does, that he will lose all his companions in the journey.
- This is where we can all stop wondering why Poseidon hates Odysseus so much.
- Polyphemos hurls another rock, this one landing behind the ship and forcing it out to sea.
- Shortly thereafter, Odysseus lands and makes a sacrifice to Zeus.
- It is rejected. (We don't really know how that works, but take Odysseus's word for it – he clearly messed with the wrong one-eyed man-eating son-of-a-god.)

Book X

- Odysseus's crew lands next on the island of Aiolia, ruled by Aiolos, the god of the winds.
- Aiolos welcomes the Ithakans and listens to their tale of the Trojan War. They stay at his home for a month.
- When they leave, the gracious Aiolos gifts Odysseus with a bag of storm winds. The idea is that only the west wind is left free to blow the Ithakans straight back home.
- Odysseus doesn't tell his men what's in the bag, and just takes care of steering the ship by himself for nine days.
- Then, expectedly, he falls asleep, exhausted. His men see Ithaka on the horizon, but before waking their master decide to check out what's in the sack; they think it may be treasure of some sort.
- This is a phenomenally bad idea.
- The moment they open the sack all the storm winds rage out and blow the ship backwards, undoing all their nine days of sailing.
- Odysseus, again expectedly, despairs. He even thinks to kill himself, which would be all suspenseful if he weren't the one telling this story.
- So instead of suicide, Odysseus rows all the way back to Aiolia and begs for more help.
- Aiolos now realizes that Odysseus is cursed by the gods, because there's no other way he could've messed that one up. The god refuses to help him.
- So the Ithakans row for six more days and again see land – Lamos, this time, the land of the Laistrygones, who are something between ogres and giants.
- When the men land, the king, Antiphates, greets them by falling on the first man and drinking his blood.
- Freaked out, Odysseus and his men leave.
- They sail again until they reach the island of Aiaia, home of the goddess Circe.
- Odysseus scouts around and sees a plume of smoke rising inland. Made cautious by his last few adventures, he decides not to explore it alone.
- Instead, after killing a big stag for dinner, he sends 22 men – including his friend Eurylochos – to explore the hall.
- The witch Circe greets them and invites them in. They are stunned by her beauty and everyone goes, except for cautious Eurylochos.
- He watches in secret as the men eat. Unfortunately, Circe has drugged the food with magic, so the men quickly turn into pigs. The witch drives them into a pigsty after dinner.
- Eurylochos runs back to the ship to warn Odysseus, who arms up to rescue his men. Eurylochos begs him not to go back, and in fact stays behind himself once the men set out

with their master.

- On the way, Odysseus is visited by the god Hermes who gives him advice to battle Circe. He gives him a magical herb called *moly*.
- Nevertheless, the god insists that Odysseus eat it to keep from turning into an animal at Circe's table. He tells the mortal to draw his sword when the witch tries to drive him into a cage. Then, when she breaks down, to agree to have sex with her if she vows not to use magic against him.
- Odysseus follows all the instructions and gets hot and heavy with the beautiful sorceress.
- Afterwards, Circe restores Odysseus's companions to him by turning them back to human form.
- Then the witch, who is apparently a nice person now, invites the whole crew to stay with her and rest, which they do. For a year. (!)
- Finally, one of Odysseus's men asks if perchance they could consider the possibility of potentially, perhaps, maybe going home.
- So Odysseus approaches Circe to help them get to Ithaka.
- She prophecies that he cannot go home until he visits the land of the dead to see the prophet Teiresias, who has further instructions for him. She gives him directions to get to the Underworld (which you could reach by ship back then, it would seem).
- Meanwhile, Elpenor – one of Odysseus's crew members – wanders to the rooftop to get some fresh air and spends the night up there.
- In the morning, Elpenor wakes up and falls off the roof to his death.
- But nobody notices because they are all despairing over the news of going to the Underworld and also they're busy preparing the ship.
- They find that Circe has disappeared for good, leaving behind only a black ewe and ram for the sacrifice required to enter the Underworld (like a highway toll, but bloodier).

Book XI

- Odysseus travels to the Underworld and makes the offerings according to Circe's instructions. The shades of the dead (shades = ghosts) gather to drink of the spilt blood and then talk to Odysseus.
- The first shade is Elpenor, freshly fallen from Circe's roof. Odysseus's eyes bug out when he sees one of his crew members – he weeps and listens to the man's story.
- Elpenor begs for Odysseus to honor his death by building a burial mound (essentially a pile of rocks) for his dead body. Odysseus agrees. It's the least he can do.
- Odysseus then glimpses his mother's shade among the rest of the dead. This is news to him, since last he heard she was still alive. Not a good way to find out.
- Fortunately, he is soon distracted from his weeping by the arrival of Teiresias (the dead blind prophet).
- Teiresias drinks the blood of Odysseus's sacrifice so he can speak with the man.
- He then warns the man of things to come; he says not to eat Helios's cattle at Thrinakia, and then casually announces that Odysseus will survive alone (in other words, all of his companions will die).
- The good news is, Odysseus will make it home after all. And there he will find…trouble. He

will have to make the suitors pay for their insolence with blood (a popular currency around these parts).

- After defeating the suitors, Teiresias continues, Odysseus must go inland until he reaches an area of earth which has never known the sea. There he must pray to Poseidon in order to ensure himself a peaceful seaborne death in his old age, surrounded by all his folk.
- After hearing all this advice, Odysseus asks Teiresias why his mother is here and if he can talk to her.
- Teiresias says sure, as long as she drinks the blood of the sacrifice, too.
- One gory mess later, Odysseus's mother Antikleia tells him of the situation back home in Ithaka, detailing Telemachos's growth but helplessness against the suitors, Penelope's loyalty and long suffering, and her own death out of loneliness for Odysseus.
- Her son tries three times to embrace her, but Antikleia is dead, so this isn't really possible.
- When she leaves, there's a long line of other dead people waiting to talk to him. The shades don't get too many visitors around these parts.
- Odysseus draws his sword to hold them back. (Except they're already dead, so we're not sure how effective that would be.) He lets them come and drink one at a time.
- Odysseus speaks first to a long line of princesses: Tyro, Antiope, Alkmene, Megara, Epikaste, Chloris, Leda, Iphimedeia, Phaidra, Prokris, Ariadne, Maira, Klymene, and Eriphyle.
- At this point, Odysseus pauses in his narrative. The Phaiakians are all "No way!"
- Queen Arete, clearly impressed by all these stories, decides that when they do finally send Odysseus on his way, it should be with lots of sparkly things (i.e., treasure).
- King Alkinoös is all, "Wait a minute, *I'm* the King around here," but he agrees about the sparkly things.
- He then asks Odysseus if, while he was down in the underworld, he met any of his friends who died at Troy.
- So Odysseus resumes his story.
- Back in the Underworld, Odysseus sees Agamemnon and hears the tragic story of his murder and his son Orestes's revenge against Aigisthos and Klytaimestra.
- Agamemnon is understandably bitter against women and considers all of them treacherous. Oh, except for Penelope, whom he praises for her loyalty. (Nice save.)
- Then appear the spirits of Achilleus, Patroklos, Antilochos, and Telamonian Aias, some of Odysseus's buddies from the Trojan war.
- Odysseus praises Achilleus for having earned so much honor and glory in his life; surely his death was like, the greatest death ever.
- Achilleus doesn't agree. Actually, he says, being dead sucks. He'd rather be a poor country farmer who is *alive* than a glorious lord in the Underworld. Wise words.
- He then asks Odysseus about his son, Neoptolemos; Odysseus responds with what he knows of the lad's brilliance and luck in battle.
- Then Odysseus pleads with Telamonian Aias to forget their earlier quarrel in Troy over Achilleus's arms.
- [Mythological Context Lesson: You've already heard about little Aias, so here's the deal with big or "Telamnonian" Aias (he's called that because he's big and his dad's name was Telamon). Back at Troy, Odysseus and big Aias competed for the arms of Achilleus, who had been killed and therefore didn't need his weapons anymore. The arms were to go to the bravest man, but the Greeks couldn't bring themselves to make a decision since they figured whoever lost would leave the war in a huff. They couldn't really afford to

anger and lose either of these great heroes, so they let the Trojan captives decide. The Trojans picked Odysseus, and the enraged Aias killed himself.]

- Clearly still peeved, the ghostly Aias turns away from Odysseus. Ouch. Rejected.
- Before he goes, Odysseus also sees Minos, Orion, Tityos, Tantalos, Sisyphos, and Herakles. These are all figures of Greek myth and, if you're interested in the specifics, check out your text.
- When all the shades come crowding in to drink the blood, Odysseus freaks out and runs back to his ship.
- Everyone leaves the Underworld, a little bit wiser and less a few sacrificial animals.

Book XII

- The Ithakans return to Aiaia, recover Elpenor's body, and go through the proper funeral rites as promised.
- Circe reappears and feeds the men. She makes them promise to stay for the full day of feasting while she gives further directions to Odysseus.
- "Further directions" seems to be a euphemism for "more sex." Still, after the "further directions," she gives some actual instructions on how to avoid the temptation of the Sirens who will try to lure him to death with their beautiful voices.
- Circe tells Odysseus that no man has ever heard the song of the Sirens and lived to tell the tale. He should have his men plug up their ears and tie him to the mast; this way he can listen yet not fall victim.
- Then she tells him about two different courses he can take to go home. The first one contains Rovers, moving rocks that are impossible for any ship to get through.
- Despite Odysseus's affinity for real-life video games, that pretty much rules out option one.
- The second route holds two dangers: Skylla, a sea monster with six heads that eats men, and Charybdis, a whirlpool that sucks and vomits out the sea three times a day.
- Amazingly, this is the better option. Circe advises Odysseus to hug the cliff of Skylla and lose six men rather than risk losing his whole ship to Charybdis. Also, he should race through as quickly as possible instead of trying to fight her (the monsters are female).
- Odysseus protests; he'd rather not lose *any* men.
- Circe tells him to suck it up.
- She then warns him not to kill Helios's cattle at Thrinakia unless he wants to lose his entire crew.
- The next day they set sail with the help of Circe's magical wind.
- The Ithakans approach the Sirens and, following Circe's instructions, Odysseus plugs his men's ears with melted beeswax and then instructs them to tie him securely to the mast so he can listen but not die.
- For the complete lyrics, please see your text, but they basically say, "'Ey you! Come 'ere!"
- Just as they successfully pass the Sirens, the men approach Skylla and Charybdis and promptly lose their oars in fear.
- Odysseus tries to inspire courage in them while he arms up against Skylla. Clearly, he's forgetting Circe's instructions.

- As foretold, Skylla takes six of Odysseus's best men. He suddenly remembers that he's supposed to move quickly rather than fight the she-monster, so his ship makes it out. Barely.
- They then see Thrinakia – land of Helios's cattle – which Odysseus wants to sail past since he's been warned against it about twelve times.
- But his men, led by Eurylochos, vote to stay there for a night's rest. They have been seriously freaked out by the trials they just faced and saddened by the friends they lost.
- Odysseus agrees to stay, but makes the men vow not to touch Helios's cattle.
- At dawn, they see an impending storm and move their ship to a protected grotto.
- It storms for a full month. Their food runs out. And they're still surrounded by Helios's cattle.
- Odysseus goes off to pray to the gods one day and finally Eurylochos snaps. He persuades the men to kill the biggest cow they can find and promises to atone for it by building a big temple to Helios once they get back to Ithaka.
- The men agree and get to cooking the cattle.
- Odysseus comes back, sees the cooking meat, and despairs...in an angsty, we're-going-to-die sort of way.
- Helios, angry at this transgression, asks Zeus for revenge. The King of the Gods promises to destroy Odysseus's ship with his thunderbolt.
- When the storm passes, the Ithakans set sail and are promptly struck by Zeus's thunderbolt.
- Everyone dies except Odysseus.
- The sea floats him back towards Skylla and Charybdis, and he manages to survive only by jumping on the huge tree-island thingy positioned above Charybdis. He clings to its trunk while Charybdis ingests his ship.
- When she spits it back up again, Odysseus let go and lands on its flotsam. The gods help him evade Skylla as he rows past her using his hands as oars.
- He drifts on the open sea for nine days before washing ashore the island of Ogygia, where Kalypso rescues him.
- But then she keeps him prisoner for seven years, which kind of negates her whole rescuer argument.
- At this point, Odysseus ends his narrative for real this time.

Book XIII

- Alkinoös, moved by Odysseus's harrowing tale, promises that each Phaiakian man will give him a gift to build up wealth for his return to Ithaka.
- They feast all the next day while Alkinoös's men prepare the ships. Odysseus is impatient to leave.
- Alkinoös's men row him to Ithaka during the night as Odysseus sleeps on the ship. (They make it look so easy!)
- They land on a rocky grotto, unload the still sleeping Odysseus, and leave him on the shore with all his treasure.
- Up in the clouds, or wherever it is that gods hang out, Poseidon sees Odysseus in Ithaka

and approaches Zeus angrily. He wants Odysseus to suffer – more! Mwah-hah-hah.

- Zeus tells him that he is a god and therefore may take his revenge against a mortal any time he wants.
- So Poseidon finds the Phaiakians' returning ship, which is in sight of its homeland, and turns it into stone, which doesn't float so much. He would like to throw up some mountains around their city as well, but Zeus says that would be overkill.
- Alkinoös, seeing this happen, remembers the prophecy we heard in Book VIII (that his ship would be turned to stone and mountains thrown up around his island if his people were nice to strangers) and promptly whacks himself on the forehead.
- Meanwhile, Athene, up to her old tricks again, conjures a grey mist to hide Odysseus while he sleeps.
- When he wakes, Odysseus doesn't recognize his home and has no idea where he is. He thinks the Phaiakians have deceived him.
- After he counts his treasure and realizes none of it is stolen, he is approached by Athene, dressed as a shepherd.
- Odysseus asks the shepherd where he is.
- Athene tells him this is Ithaka.
- When the shepherd asks him who he is, Odysseus makes up an elaborate story about being a hunted man from Crete who fought in the Trojan War and just escaped a ship of pirates.
- Athene, highly amused, reveals her true form and has a hearty laugh. Then she comments that Odysseus is indeed a master liar. Which is a compliment. We think.
- We learn that Odysseus thought himself abandoned by the goddess after the Trojan War, but is pleased to discover that she's been the one following him around and putting protective clouds over him.
- Athene reaffirms that this land is Ithaka. She lifts the protective cloud from around him so that he can see clearly that this is indeed his beloved homeland.
- He and Athene hide Odysseus's treasure safely in the grotto and plan their revenge on the suitors.
- Athene tells Odysseus she will disguise him as a beggar, because she is the master of disguises and no one likes to look too closely at beggars anyway. She orders him to go see his swineherd in the forest while she flies to Sparta to call Telemachos home.

Book XIV

- When Odysseus arrives at the swineherd's home in the forest, he is nearly attacked by the dogs.
- Luckily for him, the swineherd Eumaios saves him and then welcomes him into his hut and offers him what little food and comfort he has.
- While serving his guest, Eumaios talks all about the history of the land – King Odysseus's leaving to fight in Troy, the suitors' uncouth takeover of Odysseus's home, Penelope's staunch loyalty despite her suffering, and Telemachos's helplessness against the suitors.
- This is nothing new.
- Still disguised as a beggar, Odysseus tries to tell Eumaios that Odysseus is not dead and

will come back.

- The swineherd is skeptical.
- Then he asks the beggar about himself. Odysseus makes up an elaborate story about being a man from Crete, a commoner, who coincidentally has suffered many of the same trials that Odysseus did.
- In his made-up story, he claims to have heard news about Odysseus, who had recently left an island just when the beggar arrived. He adds that Odysseus is currently consulting an oracle and then means to return home.
- Eumaios thinks the beggar is lying. He says that Odysseus is dead at sea, but it's pretty clear that the beggar's story has planted a seed of hope.
- Eumaios brings the beggar more food, making a big deal about treating his guest as Odysseus would've wished. Beggar Odysseus is touched.
- After dinner, Odysseus wants to beg for a cloak so he can sleep, but tells a witty story instead.
- Ah, but this is the kind of story that carries a subtle message, in this case, "Give me a cloak please."
- Eumaios, who is one sharp swineherd, gets the message and gives the beggar a fine heavy cloak under which to sleep. He tells him to stay at the hut until Telemachos returns and can give him passage wherever he wishes.

Book XV

- Athene makes her way to Sparta, where Telemachos is in bed but not yet asleep. She urges him to leave immediately for Ithaka because Eurymachos is going to marry Penelope. (This is not true.)
- She advises him to go to Eumaios the swineherd as soon as he reaches Ithaka. Then he can entrust Eumaios with the news that he is home and have him go tell the queen.
- (Remember, the suitors are all ready to kill Telemachos if he shows his face, so some discretion is required.)
- All worked up by Athene's lie, Telemachos tells Peisistratos that he must leave. Still, the prince tells him to wait until dawn (which is coming shortly).
- At dawn, Menelaos rushes to get Telemachos gifts and transportation ready. Menelaos, Helen, and Peisistratos each choose a gift for him. Helen's, in particular, is touching – a beautiful gown woven by her own hands for Telemachos's future bride.
- Just as Telemachos is about to leave, Zeus sends a sign – an eagle flying with a dead farmyard goose in its talons.
- Helen interprets this to mean that the god-favored Odysseus has returned to Ithaka and will remove the household pests – the suitors – from his home.
- Telemachos and Peisistratos drive the whole day and sleep that night at Pherai.
- The following morning, Telemachos requests that Peisistratos take him straight to his ships and send word for his men to join him. He wants to avoid meeting Nestor and waiting for more gifts, which as we've seen takes forever in ancient Greece.
- Peisistratos agrees and does so.
- Just as Telemachos is about to set sail, a stranger approaches him, a descendent of

Melampous and a man gifted with prophetic abilities.

- This of course means we all need some back story. OK, so Melampous was a rich, happy Lord until King Neleus exiled him and took over his house. We don't know exactly why, other than the vague mention that it had something to do with Neleus's beautiful daughter. (The fact that this story is thrown in without a lot of details probably means Homer's readers were already familiar with it as common knowledge.)
- Melampous was held captive in his exile by yet another man, Phylakos. Somehow he escaped, took back his lands, carried off Neleus's daughter and gave her in marriage to his brother, and then, because it was his destiny, went to Argos to be ruler.
- Several generations later, Theoklymenos was born; he is the prophetic man who's asking Telemachos for a ride home. His reasons for hitchhiking are: 1) he killed his cousin in Argos, and 2) he is being hunted for the murder.
- Telemachos says sure, come on board.
- Back in Ithaka, Odysseus tests whether Eumaios will try to drive him off to the city or lavish him with more hospitality.
- Eumaios takes offense at the beggar's insinuations of being a burden and welcomes him to stay until Telemachos returns.
- Then beggar Odysseus asks for information about the Queen and Odysseus's father, Laertes.
- Eumaios reports that Laertes is alive, but wishes he were dead because he grieves so much for his son.
- We learn that Eumaios grew up as Laertes's ward in the household and was a playmate to the Princess Ktimene, Laertes daughter (who therefore was Odysseus's sister).
- When Ktimene got married and left Ithaka, Eumaios was given provisions and sent to the forest to work as a swineherd. (As far as we can tell, this wasn't intended as a punishment of any sort, though it does seem like this guy got the short end of the stick.)
- Odysseus, curious, asks Eumaios where he is from (apparently he wants more information than he just received).
- So the swineherd launches into his story.
- Eumaios reveals that he was the son of a Syrian lord and a Sidonian slave woman. His mother was unhappy as a slave and jumped at the opportunity to escape back to her homeland when some sailors whom she slept with offered her passage there.
- She took young Eumaios with her on the ship, but died barely a week into the voyage. Eumaios was sold at Ithaka to Laertes.
- Odysseus feels sorry for the guy so the two men talk night the night away and trade stories.
- Aboard Telemachos's ship, the fugitive guy Theoklymenos asks the prince where he may find lodging in Ithaka.
- Telemachos says he would offer his own house, but unfortunately it's currently occupied by swarms of suitors. He tells Theoklymenos briefly about his lost father.
- Zeus sends a sign, a hawk flying by with a dove in its talons.
- Theoklymenos interprets this to mean Odysseus's family will rule Ithaka forever.
- Telemachos asks one of his crewmen, Peiraios, if Theoklymenos can stay with him. Peiraios sportingly agrees.
- When they land in Ithaka, Telemachos makes his way to the swineherd's hut.

Book XVI

- Telemachos arrives to find Eumaios conversing with a beggar.
- Eumaios jumps up to greet Telemachos enthusiastically; it is obvious that he loves him like a son.
- Eumaios introduces the beggar to Telemachos and asks if he will lodge the old man and provide him with transport.
- Telemachos laments that his house is being intruded on, but offers the beggar clothing and food and further permission to stay with Eumaios.
- He worries aloud that he isn't trained in arms and will likely do a lousy job of ousting the suitors. (Plus, he's sort of outnumbered.)
- Odysseus/the beggar pumps his son up. He urges Telemachos to seek the aid of his brothers in ousting the suitors, adding that even if the odds are stacked against him, it's better to die in glorious battle than to be beaten by all these suitors.
- Telemachos says he has no brothers and no chance against the suitors, who are some of the toughest men in the land.
- He sends Eumaios to Penelope with the news that he has returned, but warns the swineherd not to let the suitors hear.
- When Eumaios asks if he should take the news to suffering Laertes, Telemachos tells him to let Eurykleia the nurse tell him instead. (Keep this in mind.)
- At this point, Odysseus spots Athene outside and goes to her. Telemachos cannot see her, which could possibly make for some comic relief.
- She tells Odysseus to reveal himself to Telemachos and removes his disguise with her wand.
- Telemachos is astonished by the staggering transformation and thinks Odysseus to be a god.
- While Telemachos is all overcome by wonder and happiness, Odysseus berates him for not taking the news more like a man.
- After the hugging and tears, the father and son plot to defeat the suitors. Based on Telemachos's information, there are over one hundred of them. These are some mighty high odds.
- Telemachos despairs, but Odysseus tells him to have faith – after all, the gods are on their side. (Well, except for that one god…) Both Athene and Zeus, he says, will aid them against the suitors.
- Odysseus outlines the plan: tomorrow, Athene will disguise him as the beggar again for him to go to the royal hall. He will distract the suitors while Telemachos moves their weapons into another room and locks them up.
- Odysseus has set aside only two swords, spears, and shields for their own use. Other than that, they're trusting in the gods to assist them.
- He also warns Telemachos not to let anyone else know that he has returned.
- The pair agrees to question the female servants of the household to discover which ones are loyal to their cause.
- Then they send a runner to the Queen with the information saying that Telemachos has returned.
- This not so smart for two reasons: one, they already sent Eumaios to do just that; and two, this runner shouts the news aloud so that everyone, including the suitors, hears.

- Twenty minutes later, Eumaios tells the queen in private that her son has returned, and she's all, "No kidding."
- Back at the royal hall, the seabound suitors return to their friends, clearly having failed to ambush and kill Telemachos. They're mad.
- Antinoös urges the suitors to act quickly. Now that everyone knows they've tried to kill Telemachos, they might as well strike the first blow.
- Another (and more prudent) suitor named Amphinomos isn't quite so trigger-happy: he advises them to pray to the gods to see if they are favored. The others agree.
- Meanwhile, Medon, our favorite the town crier, has overheard the suitors' plans yet again and brings the info to Penelope.
- She confronts the suitors and accuses them of trying to kill her son.
- Eurymachos is all, "Who, us? Never!" and the Queen, who is helpless because she is a woman, goes upstairs.
- Back at the hut, Athene again disguises Odysseus – just as Eumaios returns. He delivers the news that a crier ruined their secrecy and that he spotted an unknown ship coming to Ithaka. (It's implied that this is the ship of the unsuccessful ambushing suitors.)
- Still, Odysseus and Telemachos aren't worried. They eat their dinner in peace and go to sleep.

Book XVII

- Telemachos wakes and says that he must go to town so Penelope can see with her own eyes that he is in fact alive. He leaves orders that Eumaios is to bring "the beggar" to town during the day so that he can beg for food.
- Back in the great hall, Penelope is ecstatic to see her son alive. She asks him for news of Odysseus, but Telemachos tells her to be patient.
- Penelope complies.
- Telemachos then orders her to go bathe, change her clothes, and pray that Zeus will help them with their revenge against the suitors. He leaves with the excuse that he must take care of a passenger who unexpectedly sailed with him yesterday.
- Telemachos quickly spots Odysseus's loyal friends – Mentor (the real one this time), Antiphos, and Halitherses – and goes off to consult with them.
- Periaios brings Theoklymenos to Telemachos and asks the prince to send some maids so that they can get Menelaos's gifts into the house. Telemachos prudently tells him to wait and keep the treasure for now until they can be sure the suitors won't touch it.
- Peiraios obeys and leaves with his guest.
- The men enjoy a meal while Penelope weaves. She asks her son again for news of Odysseus, this time taking a firmer stance.
- Telemachos tells her the truth about his visit with Menelaos, but omits the fact that Odysseus is home. He only gives her faint hope by telling her what Proteus revealed to Menelaos – that Odysseus was last seen alive on the island of Kalypso.
- Theoklymenos interrupts and tells Penelope about the sign he interpreted for Telemachos the day before – the sign which prophecies that Odysseus is in fact *already* back in Ithaka and plotting revenge.

- To Telemachos's relief, Penelope doesn't believe the prophet's words. Phew. That was a close one.
- Medon, the town crier, calls the suitors (who are playing sports and engaging in other manly pursuits) to come in for dinner.
- While they're busy filing in, Odysseus – still in the guise of a beggar – leaves the forest with Eumaios and heads to town, even using a walking stick to play up his disguise.
- Eventually, the pair runs into Melanthios the annoying goatherd. He mocks the beggar, tells him to go home, and even kicks at him.
- Odysseus doesn't respond, though he burns with rage inside. All he does is pray aloud to the gods that Melanthios gets what he deserves. Given what we've seen so far, we're about 98% sure this will in fact happen.
- We find out that Melanthios willingly serves Eurymachos and adores him.
- When they reach the hall, Eumaios asks the beggar to stay at the entrance and allow him to enter first. Odysseus agrees.
- As the disguised Odysseus speaks, an old dog sitting on a dung heap nearby pricks his ears up and tries to wag his tail.
- Odysseus recognizes him as Argos, the hound that he trained as a puppy but never had the chance to take hunting before he left for Troy. Now poor Argos is old and mistreated by everyone, which is kind of sad.
- Odysseus sheds a tear for the poor condition of his favorite dog and inquires about the animal.
- Eumaios says that Odysseus owned this dog; the animal was swift, strong, and courageous in his prime, but now he's just abused by everyone.
- As the men enter the hall, Argos breathes his last breath and dies happy, having recognized and seen his master after twenty years.
- Eumaios grabs a spare bench and seats himself across from Telemachos while the disguised Odysseus enters the hall.
- Telemachos, who has to pretend he doesn't know this guy, gives the beggar a generous hunk of bread and meat and tells him not to be shy in asking for food.
- Odysseus goes down the line, begging food from each man. With this strategy, he learns who among the suitors goes on the good list and who on the naughty list.
- This would be a great way to decide who lives and who perishes, if Athene didn't command that everyone has to die, which she does.
- Everyone gives Odysseus something until Melanthios recognizes him as the same old beggar from before; he again insults the man.
- After hearing this, Antinoös turns on Eumaios and scolds him for bringing a beggar to the hall.
- OK, so we've got two names for our naughty list…
- Telemachos stops Eumaios from his angry reply, but only so he can insult Antinoös himself. He commands the suitor to give the beggar some bread.
- Antinoös threatens to instead throw a footstool at the man. But beggar Odysseus ignores him.
- After he has begged and received from everyone else, Odysseus calls on Antinoös to give something. He begins by telling him a false sob story of how he was a rich man once and had the misfortune to sail to Egypt.
- Antinoös interrupts with a refusal to feed him.
- Beggar Odysseus insults him: he says it's a shame that Antinoös looks so much more

lordly than he is.
- Zing!
- Enraged, Antinoös throws a footstool at the beggar (in his defense, he *did* give fair warning) and clips him on the shoulder. Odysseus doesn't even wince, but inwardly rages to return the favor.
- Everyone is embarrassed by Antinoös's uncouth behavior; some loudly reprimand him for striking a poor beggar.
- Upstairs, Penelope hears all the noise and can tell that Antinoös is causing trouble again. She sends her maid to fetch the beggar to her for questioning – she wants to ask him for any news on Odysseus.
- Eumaios takes the message to beggar Odysseus, who says that he will meet with the Queen later tonight; he wants to avoid any suspicion from the suitors.
- Penelope, at first desperate to hear this news, eventually calms down and realizes that this is a clever beggar.
- Eumaios leaves to tend to the herds as the banquet continues.

Book XVIII

- A real beggar by the name of Iros, who regularly begs at Odysseus's hall, sees the newcomer and rudely demands that he get out. Clearly, this town isn't big enough for *two* beggars.
- Odysseus tries to reason with the man, but he is staunch. This launches us into another back-and-forth round of insults.
- Antinoös, seeing these two going at each other, spurs them on, since everyone loves a good fight. He promises a prize of fat blood pudding to the winner.
- Telemachos assures beggar Odysseus that the crowd will watch his back (meaning they won't let some jerk hit him with a footstool). The crowd cheers, proving that if there's one thing Greeks can agree on, it's that old beggars shouldn't be hit unawares from behind.
- Iros is all, "You're going down!" and Odysseus is all, "Oh really? Well look at…THIS!" and then he rips off his shirt and everyone goes "Ooooh!"
- Antinoös, noting Iros's fear, threatens to have him beaten and castrated if the new beggar wins against him.
- Odysseus decides to be merciful and strike Iros only once, which he does, in the jaw. Unfortunately for Iros, this one punch is enough to break his jaw. Blood proceeds to do what it always does in the *Odyssey*, namely, spew everywhere.
- Everyone is massively entertained by the fight and they all cheer the beggar Odysseus on.
- Amphinomos, who we've already seen is a not-so-bad suitor, gets some advice from the beggar, who urges the suitor to go home before Odysseus returns and punishes everyone by exacting some revenge.
- Amphinomos is convinced, but Athene will not allow him to leave – she wants *all* the suitors to die.
- Moving on to less vindictive activities, Athene puts Penelope to sleep for a few minutes during which she showers her in ambrosia and makes her even lovelier than she already is.

- The goddess inspires Penelope to show herself to the suitors and get them all hot and bothered over her. The Queen makes her appearance with the excuse of berating Telemachos for allowing such poor treatment of the beggar.
- Indeed, Penelope proceeds to have a model moment in front of all the suitors, who appreciate it wholeheartedly.
- Penelope is oblivious to her influence on the men and scolds Telemachos for allowing such abuse (she's referring to the beggar) in her household.
- Telemachos replies that it was not what it seemed.
- Eurymachos interrupts and compliments Penelope on her beauty. Though she plays modest at first, Penelope finally ends up flirting a bit with the suitors; she complains that they haven't courted her correctly, as not one of them has presented her with any gifts.
- Unfortunately, not one of the suitors responds with the clearly invited line, "I've got a gift for you, come here and I'll show it to you."
- While the suitors comically search each of their troves to find a suitable gift for the Queen, Odysseus watches, highly amused.
- When Penelope leaves, her servants carrying the shining gifts she has just received, Odysseus decides to test the loyalty of her maids.
- At night, the maids are assigned to keep the torches burning in the hallway so that the suitors – getting drunk in the hall – can see what they're smacking into before they smack into it.
- Beggar Odysseus tells the servants he'll take care of the torches tonight and sends them up to go care for Penelope.
- The women giggle at him. One girl, Melantho, calls him crazy or drunk for sticking around with the drunk and rowdy suitors.
- Beggar Odysseus threatens to tell Telemachos about their rude behavior, so the girls scatter in fear.
- The suitors, seeing the beggar tending the torches, begin teasing him again. Odysseus answers in kind, boasting that he could defeat any of them in battle.
- This infuriates Eurymachos, and he lobs a footstool at the beggar. Very original. It misses, however, and hits a wine steward, spilling all the wine.
- Amphinomos restores the peace by turning their attention to the banquet and away from the fighting. They all go back to eating.
- And getting drunk.

Book XIX

- Odysseus, still disguised as the beggar, commands Telemachos to remove the suitors' weapons from the great hall, as planned.
- Telemachos tells Eurykleia to go shut the women in their rooms while he does so. Again, this won't be suspicious at all.
- Odysseus and Telemachos move the weapons together, their path lit by Athene, who is conveniently bearing a torch for the occasion.
- For the first time, it seems, Telemachos realizes just how deeply Athene is invested in helping Odysseus. He is awed.

- Penelope sits on her chair in her room, awaiting the beggar to come as promised.
- Melantho sees Odysseus coming up and insults him; he replies that she should think about what Odysseus would think of her behavior.
- Penelope rushes to his aid and dismisses the maid.
- The Queen asks the beggar where he is from, but he replies that the topic is too painful to discuss. Instead, he gets information from her.
- She tells him about the long years she has spent waiting for her husband to return and how she tricked the suitors with her shroud-weaving routine.
- But now she is desperate and has given up hope. She plans to marry a suitor soon, just to get out of Telemachos's house and let him live in peace. (Nooo!)
- Finally, she persuades the beggar to tell her about himself. Odysseus assumes a fake name – Aithon – and weaves a complex story in which he came from Crete, fought in Troy, and later played host to Odysseus.
- Penelope gets excited at hearing her husband's name, but doubts the truth of his tale; she asks for details about Odysseus's appearance – just to make sure.
- The beggar describes Odysseus's clothing, weapons, and men perfectly, moving Penelope to tears.
- He goes on to promise her that Odysseus is returning. In fact, he claims, he will be back...today!
- But Penelope remains unconvinced.
- Still, she offers the man a bath, clothes, and bed for the night.
- The beggar, however, refuses the bath (which is really just a foot washing) unless he gets it from a maid as old and long-suffering as he is.
- Playing right into his hands, Penelope offers the services of Eurykleia, Odysseus's nurse when he was young.
- Eurykleia notices the strong resemblance between the beggar and Odysseus, but the beggar brushes it off by saying he gets that a lot.
- She begins washing his feet.
- Odysseus realizes something and freezes – he must not let her see the scar on his thigh. (Thigh!? Just what kind of foot wash is this, anyway?)
- Flashback to the scar story: as a boy Odysseus went on a hunt on Mount Parnassos with his grandfather Autolykos, where he was gashed in the thigh by a wild boar. It left an unmistakable scar.
- Of course, Eurykleia spots the mark, knows the man to be Odysseus, and freaks out.
- Odysseus whispers to the old woman, so as not to alert the nearby Queen, and vows her to silence – especially with respect to Penelope.
- Eurykleia promises to zip it.
- In the meantime, Penelope, utterly oblivious, asks the beggar one last question. She describes to him a dream she had in which she joyfully watched the domestic geese in her garden. Sweet, until a mountain eagle swooped down and killed them all.
- She and her attendant women began to wail in sorrow, but the eagle came back and spoke, saying that he is her lord returned and the geese are the suitors.
- We wish all our dreams interpreted themselves for us.
- Still, this isn't enough explanation for Penelope. She asks the beggar to interpret the dream...again.
- The beggar tells her it means certain death for the suitors.
- Penelope is still doubtful.

- She tells him that she is so tired of the courtship that she will end it tomorrow by issuing a contest in which the suitors must string Odysseus's old bow and shoot an arrow through twelve consecutive axe heads. She will marry the suitor who wins it.
- The beggar promises that Odysseus will be present for the contest.
- Still skeptical, Penelope goes upstairs to sleep.

Book XX

- Beggar Odysseus settles down to bed on the floor outside of Penelope's room, but has trouble falling asleep. Kind of like before the night of a big game, or in this case the slaughter of 100+ men.
- He sees some of the maids slipping out to go sleep with the suitors. He is enraged at the maids' betrayal but stays silent.
- Athene arrives and instructs Odysseus to have faith.
- Meanwhile, upstairs, Penelope is crying for Odysseus. She prays to Artemis for death rather than more of this endless suffering. She dreams that Odysseus comes back, but of course doesn't believe the good omen.
- Odysseus wakes at dawn and, in a moment of angst, asks Zeus for a sign that he was meant to come home.
- Zeus hears and sends a thunderclap through a perfectly clear sky.
- A maid grinding barley hears the thunder clap and knows Zeus must be around and listening. She prays that all her hard work to feed the greedy suitors will soon be over. Oh, and that all the suitors die. This is convenient for Zeus, who gets to grant two prayers at once.
- And we're back to Odysseus, who takes heart at seeing the thunderbolt.
- Telemachos checks up on beggar Odysseus and then orders the maids to prepare a feast, because today is a holiday.
- Melanthios returns to taunt the beggar more. Does he ever learn? And also, doesn't he have anything else to do?
- Afterwards another man approaches the beggar – Philoitios, the resident cowherd. He greets the beggar warmly and notes his resemblance to Odysseus. We quickly see that he is ashamed and outraged at the suitors' behavior in his lord's house.
- The beggar asks Eumaios and Philoitios if they would fight on Odysseus's side against the suitors should he return to Ithaka. They both eagerly answer yes.
- The suitors, at the sound of breakfast, drop all their plans of killing Telemachos and turn their minds to the real task at hand – eating.
- Telemachos seats the beggar opposite himself with his own share of food and a goblet of wine and challenges anyone to insult him.
- For the most part, no one does, although there is some mild grumbling from (surprise) Antinoös.
- We find out that the "holiday" is really a day of sacrifice to Apollo.
- Athene, who apparently loves conflict, wants the suitors to tease Odysseus so he'll get all worked into a rage. Because she always gets her way, the suitors indeed taunt the beggar, one by one.

- Eventually, one suitor, Ktesippos, throws a cow's foot at the beggar. Odysseus ducks, which foils Ktesippos's mean plan.
- Telemachos, enraged, rushes to the beggar's defense.
- Yet another suitor, Agelaos, gets everyone off the topic of the beggar and back to the issue at hand: who's going to get Penelope. He asks Telemachos to see reason: it's obvious that Odysseus isn't coming back, so Penelope needs to get over herself already and marry one of the suitors. He asks that Telemachos reason with his mother.
- Telemachos refuses and the suitors laugh at him. Athene, who still wants to see some blood, makes his refusal seem *especially* hilarious to the suitors so they laugh for a *really* long time.
- Theoklymenos, the prophetic fugitive whom Telemachos gave a ride home from Pylos, has a vision of the hall filled with dripping blood and shades of the dead. Then he tells everyone about it.
- You would think this would dampen the mood, but no, the suitors just laugh at him, too.
- Telemachos rolls his eyes and tries to ignore them the best he can, a task made easier by the knowledge that, very soon, the hall will indeed be filled with their dripping blood.

Book XXI

- Penelope takes Odysseus's bow down from its special framed locale on the wall. She remembers how he obtained it as the payment for a debt from Iphitos from Lakedaimon.
- Don't worry – Homer tells you the story: Odysseus met Iphitos in Messene, where he (Odysseus) had come claiming the natives owed Ithaka for having stolen some sheep way back when. Iphitos was also there on the account of livestock; he was tracking some stray mares that apparently wandered to Messene themselves.
- Homer mentions that these very mares ended up being the death of Iphitos, since, after Messene and meeting Odysseus, he wandered to the house of Herakles (Hercules), who promptly killed him so he could have the mares.
- The point is, Odysseus became friends with Iphitos; he gave him a sword and spear, and Iphitos in return gave him the bow that Penelope is now taking off the wall.
- Back to the Queen; she approaches the suitors and announces the contest and all its details which we've already heard.
- Eumaios and Philoitios present the weapons and both break down in tears, since they know Penelope has given up hope that her husband will ever return.
- Antinoös mocks them for their sniveling.
- Telemachos is the first to try stringing the bow, not because he wants to marry his mother, but because he wants to prove his strength, manliness, and virility.
- After four tries, it looks like Telemachos is finally about to succeed – when beggar Odysseus signals for him not to do it.
- Telemachos obeys and hands the bow over to the first suitor, who fails miserably.
- Antinoös orders Melanthios to build a fire and bring a cake of lard so that they can limber up the bow in the hopes of stringing it. (Cheating!)
- As he does, beggar Odysseus notices Eumaios and Philoitios leaving the hall. He rushes after them and reveals himself as Odysseus. As proof, he shows them his scar. They

rejoice and jump to help him.

- In the meantime, Eurymachos has been shamed by the bow; he can't string it, either.
- To delay his own attempt, Antinoös distracts everyone's attention with the feast and says he will try the bow tomorrow after they have eaten.
- Beggar Odysseus speaks up; he wants a chance at stringing the bow.
- The suitors, especially Antinoös, all deny him, fearing in their hearts that he can actually do it (mostly because they've seen his absolutely awesome body a few days prior).
- Penelope scolds Antinoös and Eurymachos for treating the beggar so badly and invites him to give it a shot.
- Telemachos uncharacteristically steps forward and tells his mother that this is a man's affair and she ought to go upstairs and be a woman. Alone. In the bedroom.
- Penelope obeys, marveling at Telemachos's sudden bravery.
- As the beggar takes his time feeling the bow, Telemachos tells Eurykleia to shut all the women in their rooms and tell them not to come out until summoned, even if they hear sounds of battle.
- As the beggar takes his time stringing the bow, the suitors shout insults at him…
- …Until he successfully strings the bow in one easy motion, grabs an arrow and shoots it straight through the twelve axe heads.
- In the silence that follows, Zeus sends a sign of his favor – a single thunderclap.
- Telemachos arms himself and moves to stand next to his now unmasked father. Odysseus is back.

Book XXII

- Odysseus kills Antinoös first with an arrow to the throat. Antinoös was drinking wine at the moment of death.
- Odysseus calls out to the panicking suitors that justice has come for their lack of decorum and their impiety towards the gods.
- Realizing that their weapons are gone, the suitors scatter.
- Eurymachos begs for Odysseus to have mercy on the rest of the suitors, now that he's killed the worst of them (that would be Antinoös).
- Odysseus refuses.
- Eurymachos tries to rally the suitors to fight Odysseus, who responds by promptly killing Eurymachos with an arrow to the heart.
- As Amphinomos rushes Odysseus, Telemachos stops him with a spear to the heart.
- Telemachos then runs to the storage room, grabbing more weapons, and arming the four allies (Odysseus, himself, Eumaios, and Philoitios).
- Melanthios sees Telemachos go to the storage room and quickly does the same in order to arm the suitors.
- Odysseus is none-too-happy to see that the suitors suddenly have weapons.
- Telemachos knows it's his fault for leaving the storage room door open and confesses it to Odysseus. The King orders the two herdsmen to follow Melanthios, tie him up, and lock him in the storage room so he can do no more harm. They obey.
- All right, less apologizing/ordering and more fighting, OK guys? Especially since the suitors

now have Odysseus and Co. cornered and incredibly outnumbered.

- Athene arrives, disguised as Mentor. Odysseus recognizes her for who she is and calls help.
- The suitors beg Mentor/Athene not to help Odysseus, threatening him with death if he does.
- She turns to Odysseus and tells him to show the suitors his stuff (i.e., the skills he used against Troy) – justice, she says, is on the way.
- Still, she doesn't help just yet. Odysseus and Telemachos have yet to prove themselves worthy of her assistance. She watches her two little pet mortals from the roof and passively protects them while they pick off suitors one by one.
- At last, Athene's sign – the aegis or "great shield" – shines in the air in the hall and the suitors realize that Odysseus has godly help. They panic. Some beg for mercy, but Odysseus is ruthless.
- So ruthless, in fact, that he spares only Phemios the singer and Medon the town crier. Telemachos swears they are loyal.
- Finally, all the suitors are dead. Bloodbath? Check. Revenge? Check.
- Odysseus calls for Eurykleia to bring all the unfaithful maids to him.
- Eurykleia is all, "Um, how 'bout putting on some non-bloodbath clothes first?", and Odysseus is all, "No."
- Of the fifty maids in the household, twelve have proved disloyal. Odysseus forces them to drag the corpses of the suitors outside and clean the hall.
- He orders his son to then hack the disgraceful women to pieces outside, but Telemachos thinks this is too noble a death for these "sluts." Instead, he hangs them, which is apparently worse than being hacked to pieces.
- Then the good guys torture and kill Melanthios.
- Odysseus orders Eurykleia to bring brimstone, a brazier, and medicinal herbs so he can purify the great hall.
- Again, she tries to get him to clean up first, but he is staunch. She obeys.
- Odysseus purifies the hall, and all the maids and servants who remain with many hugs and tears (and grimaces, because as far as we can tell, he's still wearing his bloody clothes).

Book XXIII

- Eurykleia goes to Penelope with the news that Odysseus is back.
- Penelope doesn't believe her, thinking she's gone mad. Still stubborn. (Plus, did she not hear that battle going down?)
- Even when Eurykleia tells her that all the suitors are dead, Penelope thinks it must be some strange hero who has come to deliver her, not her husband.
- Still, the stubborn woman finally comes down from her room and sees Odysseus. Now she can finally accept the fact that he's back.
- Penelope doesn't accept the fact that he's back, because thinks her eyes are lying to her.
- Telemachos begs her to talk to the man, but Penelope insists that if this were Odysseus, he would know their secret signs.
- Odysseus smiles knowingly.
- Because he's worried about facing repercussions for killing all the noblemen of the country, he orders that the household keep the slaughter of the suitors a secret from the

- rest of Ithaka.
- He has a brilliant plan: they'll plan a dancing feast tonight so they can pretend that all the noise was just Penelope's wedding!
- As Odysseus is cleaning himself up, Athene makes him more handsome to the eye. (Another goddess makeover.)
- When Odysseus sits down beside Penelope that night, she is still cold towards him. She tells him that he can sleep outside her room, on the bed that Odysseus carved years ago.
- At this point Odysseus snaps, asking who dared move his bed. He rants on, raving that he built the entire bedroom around a huge olive tree and carved the bed straight from the roots; it was therefore impossible to move.
- This is the secret that Penelope referenced earlier; she rushes into Odysseus's arms in tears and begs his forgiveness for being so skeptical.
- The two rejoice, make love, and exchange stories of the twenty long years, except we're betting there are certain bits Odysseus leaves out, such as sleeping with Circe, having sex with Kalypso for seven years, and that offer of marriage to Nausikaa.
- Athene makes time go slower so that the couple can enjoy their night together and still get enough sleep.
- The following morning, Odysseus announces that he will visit his grieving father.
- He orders the women to go upstairs and lock themselves up to stay safe from any potential avengers from town; he knows that news of the slaughter will circulate fast.
- Odysseus takes Telemachos and his faithful herdsmen with him to see Laertes. Athene adds her protection by hiding them in…yes, you got it, a cloud shaped oddly like a group of traveling men.

Book XXIV

- In the meantime, the suitors' ghosts are being led by Hermes to the Underworld.
- There, the shades of Achilleus and Agamemnon exchange their stories about the Trojan War. Actually, Achilleus talks about the Trojan war, Agamemnon is still rattling on about getting killed by his unfaithful wife and her lover.
- When they see the suitors' shades entering, Agamemnon asks why they are here.
- And we get a three minute version of everything we've just read, courtesy of a suitor named Amphimedon, who amazingly blames everything on Penelope.
- Agamemnon rejoices for Odysseus, happy that the man has such a faithful wife. Unlike his own.
- Back in the land of the living, Odysseus reaches Laertes's garden lands; he sends Telemachos and the herdsmen up to the hut to prepare a good meal.
- Odysseus finds his father alone, ragged, and plowing the land dejectedly. He decides to test him to see if he is still loyal. We would expect nothing less from Odysseus at this point.
- Odysseus insults Laertes's appearance and then says his name is Quarrelman and he once housed Odysseus on his journey home.
- Laertes is grateful to the man for helping his son, but is convinced that Odysseus is dead. He obviously fell for the story that the screams of agony coming from the palace were mere wedding noises.

- Finally, Odysseus gives up the ruse and throws his arms around his father, confessing who he really is.
- Laertes… doesn't believe him. He wants proof. Odysseus shows him his thigh scar.
- Their reunion is very emotional.
- They go back to the farmhouse where the other men have prepared a meal. Laertes is joyous and Athene makes him look young again.
- When listening to Odysseus's story about defeating the suitors, Laertes wishes he could have fought alongside his son.
- Meanwhile, in town, people have heard about the massive slaughter of yesterday in Odysseus's hall. That brilliant wedding cover-up didn't work at all.
- Eupeithes clamors for revenge before the council and is approved.
- Odysseus's friends – Phemios, Medon, and Halitherses – tell the council that the gods are on Odysseus's side and warn the townspeople not to spill blood over this.
- But Eupeithes, an old man who, it turns out, is the late Antinoös's father, wants Odysseus to die. He was wins the council over. Not-so-smart men.
- In the heavens, Athene approaches Zeus to ask whether it is his will that blood be shed in revenge.
- Zeus replies that peace can only come about by mutual contract and agreement; in other words, the people must accept Odysseus as king.
- The townspeople march to Laertes's land, armed to kill Odysseus.
- Odysseus's friends stand as one. Laertes is proud to be among them.
- Telemachos invokes Athene's aid, casts his spear, and hits Eupeithes right in the helmet.
- His spear goes *through* the helmet and cleanly kills the man.
- Athene shouts for the skirmish to end and the people stop, scared by the goddess who apparently got past her desire for blood and vengeance and now is all about peace.
- She orders Odysseus to stop the battle or Zeus will be angry, leading us to believe she didn't really *listen* to Zeus's words at all.
- Odysseus obeys and both parties swear to peace with Athene as their witness.
- Finally, there is peace on Ithaka.

Themes

Theme of Fate and Free Will

In the *Odyssey*, fate and free will are not mutually exclusive concepts. Men may be destined to specific ends, but their personal choices alter the road they take to get there. The same freedom applies to the gods, who have a lot of leaway in how they bring about what is fated. Because the gods of ancient Greece are endowed with human characteristics, their will is subject to the same fickle and petty attributes of human emotion. Because of this hodge-podge of factors, the Greeks had a very different view from the one we have in mind when we think of destiny as fixed and constant.

Questions About Fate and Free Will

1. It's clear that Odysseus is responsible for his own actions and their results. It's also clear that certain events are fated to happen from the start. How are both of these possible in the *Odyssey*?
2. What is the difference between "fate" and "luck" in the *Odyssey*? When do the characters ascribe events to the former, and when to the latter, and why?
3. At what point does divine intervention strip the characters of their ability to act and think for themselves? Can we draw much of a line between, say, the ideas that Athene puts in Odysseus's head and the ideas that he devises on his own?
4. Why does Poseidon persist in harassing Odysseus if he is destined to go home? What might he gain from pursuing a seemingly futile endeavor?

Chew on Fate and Free Will

Odysseus's men brought about their own dooms by killing the sacred cattle of Helios; they deserved the deaths dealt to them.

Odysseus's men did not deserve death; they were merely innocent victims of circumstance.

Theme of Piety

Piety in the *Odyssey* is shown by deference to the gods, submission to their will, and through gestures such as sacrifices, festivals, banquets, and prayers. It also entails respect for the dead – proper burials and rites. Impiety or direct challenges to the gods often result in suffering or death for the offender.

Questions About Piety

1. Why do the gods put such importance on the living respecting the dead? In other words, are the dead more god-like than the living?
2. How are the suitors – in taking advantage of Odysseus's house in his absence – committing a crime against the gods?
3. How is piety rewarded? What specific cases of divine intervention represent a boon from the gods for proper respect paid earlier?

Chew on Piety

Although the men in the *Odyssey* revere the gods, that respect is not returned; the gods have little value for human life and often use men as their playthings.

In speaking of Odysseus, the people of Ithaka refer to him in language usually reserved for gods; they equate him with godliness, as does Homer, which is why those who disrespect him suffer the same consequences as those who are impious.

Theme of Justice

Justice is ruthless in the *Odyssey*. Death is served easily for many transgressions, from inhospitality to poor manners to disrespecting the gods. Actually, because the gods were supposed to uphold standards in daily life such as hospitality, violating those rules was itself an offence against the gods. Once it comes to meting out punishment for such offenses, Homer's characters pull very few punches.

Questions About Justice

1. What kind of justice system do the gods follow? What kinds of transgressions are punishable by death?
2. Wait a minute, is there a system at all? If the gods are subject to the same whims, grudges, desires, and pettiness as the mortals, isn't "justice" (and especially "divine justice") as inconstant and illogical as basic emotion?
3. Why does Athene want all the suitors to die – even the sort-of-cute-and-fuzzy ones? Is this "justice" according to the *Odyssey*?
4. How are chance events like Elpenor's death justified?
5. Is justice in the ancient Greek system a cover for personal vengeance? Is it fair? Are there any instances of more civil methods of punishment and reconciliation? What about the ending?

Chew on Justice

Poseidon is unjustified in hounding Odysseus across the seas because his son Polyphemos deserved the blinding that the hero gave him.

Poseidon is justified in hounding Odysseus across the seas because although Polyphemos deserved the blinding he got, Odysseus's hubris offended the gods and earned him Poseidon's enmity.

Theme of Pride

If Odysseus has one flaw, it is his pride. The hero can't take an insult lying down and insists on flaunting his victories even once challenges or battles have passed. The danger of pride in the *Odyssey* comes with the problem of angering the gods; humility was a must for the mortals, who must always remember that there are inferior to the divine.

Questions About Pride

1. Is pride mainly destructive or constructive in the *Odyssey*?
2. What is the difference between humility and straight-up weakness in the *Odyssey*? Which does Telemachos display? Is the answer to this question the same at the beginning of the epic as it is at the end?

Chew on Pride

Odysseus is often justified in showing his pride because he has the goods – muscle, courage, and an honorable name – to back it up.

No character in the *Odyssey* can afford to have hubris; by implicitly comparing the bearer to the divine, it constitutes an offense against the gods.

Theme of Lies and Deceit

Disguise is often a tool of the gods in the *Odyssey*, used to manipulate human events and test the character of mortals. But more importantly, Odysseus himself is famous for his cunning. From the Trojan horse to the clever blinding of the Cyclops, Odysseus survives and succeeds for his ability to dissemble and fool. Deception, then, is not always a negative notion in the *Odyssey*, but rather can be a means to more positive ends.

Questions About Lies and Deceit

1. For what purposes is deception used in the *Odyssey*? Are these mainly benevolent or malevolent?
2. Odysseus's cunning certainly gets him out of some tight spots, but does it ever work against him?
3. Which sex – male or female – is most associated with cunning and trickery? Which characters exemplify this? Which characters buck this trend?

Chew on Lies and Deceit

Odysseus's cunning is overrated since much of his cleverness comes through Athene's inspiration or advice.

Although Odysseus receives invaluable help and protection from Athene, his genius is his own; most of the time, he is the one to find his own way out of trouble.

Theme of Tradition and Custom

In an accurate reflection of ancient Greek culture, rules of hospitality are among the most revered social and religious laws in the *Odyssey*. Men are measured by the way they play host or guest, and those that antagonize the hero often do so by failing their part of this important contract. Guests are expected to bring gifts to their host, respect the house and servants, and act with grace and appreciation. Often, the guest is a source of news and bearings from the outside world and expected, in some ways, to sing for his supper. The host is then to provide food, shelter, and even money and transportation if the guest is in need. Breaking these obligations in the *Odyssey* is disrespectful to the gods and indicates a somewhat subhuman status.

Questions About Tradition and Custom

1. Who violates hospitality laws more severely, the suitors by their greed, or Kalypso by holding Odysseus captive?
2. The Phaiakians are the epitome of good hospitality in the *Odyssey*, yet they are punished by a god for their actions. How is this possibly just? Is this an argument against hospitality?
3. How is the concept of hospitality related to the gods? Why might piety be so closely related to good hospitality?

Chew on Tradition and Custom

Because they violated the laws of hospitality, according to the world depicted in the *Odyssey*, both Polyphemos and the suitors got what they deserved.

The Phaiakians' remarkable hospitality towards Odysseus was ultimately not worth all the trouble it caused.

Theme of Suffering

In Greek mythology, being human entails suffering. There is no escape from pain; it is the curse of mortality. Again and again in the *Odyssey*, our hero is reminded of this fact. To endure, then, is the only solution. Suffering comes in all forms in this epic, from physical pain to loneliness, isolation, and the emotional anguish of not knowing whether loved ones are alive or dead.

Questions About Suffering

1. From the gods' perspective, is there any way for mortals to avoid suffering in the *Odyssey*?
2. How do men in this epic rid themselves of pain and suffering? What about Odysseus, specifically?
3. Antikleia, Odysseus's mother, dies "out of grief" over her son's absence. How is this action depicted in the *Odyssey* – as understandable or as unwarranted?
4. Is there a point to all of Odysseus's suffering? Does he perhaps return to Ithaka humbler? Wiser?
5. Obviously, mortals suffer in the *Odyssey*. What about the gods? Is their suffering less? Different?
6. Does Penelope suffer more for her ignorance about her husband's fate than if he had simply died in the Trojan war?

Chew on Suffering

Odysseus's great suffering at sea is fair because of the injustice he committed in regards to Poseidon's son.

Suffering serves no purpose in the *Odyssey* and is merely the senseless burden that all mortals must bear.

Theme of Principles

In the *Odyssey*, respect and reputation are won in several ways. Key among them is the display of courage in battle. It is also important to honor one's hosts, guests, and the dead. At times, it is even crucial to indulge the enemy's requests, especially when it involves royalty or their dead. Because many of the qualities valued in the world of the *Odyssey* relate to domestic life as well, women could also win glory for excellence in upholding them. Still, questions are raised in the *Odyssey* as to the value of glory – especially when it comes at the expense of one's death. The epic's end, however, does seem to reaffirm the value of honor at all costs.

Questions About Principles

1. How does a man win honor in the *Odyssey*? How does a woman?
2. What characteristics define honor in the ancient Greek tradition, at least as far as you can tell from this epic?
3. How does desire for glory sometimes interfere with one's reputation or sense of honor? Think about the deaths of Telamonian Aias and Little Aias.
4. Why must Elpenor's wishes be honored? What kind of glory does he win by having Odysseus give him a proper burial? Isn't he already dead? Who cares?
5. Is "honor" a human concept in the *Odyssey*, or one handed down from the gods?
6. Why does Odysseus's lack of compassion and mercy for the suitors prove *not* to be a blow to his honor?

Chew on Principles

Odysseus is obligated to avenge himself on the suitors in order to restore honor to his house.

Theme of Loyalty

Loyalty is tricky in the *Odyssey*. While our hero is delayed sailing home from war, his wife's faithfulness is a beacon of steadfast devotion. On the other hand, Odysseus himself engages in multiple affairs before returning to his wife. Because of the cultural double-standard, the *Odyssey* doesn't condemn its hero for doing so. This raises interesting questions of different types of loyalty: one of Odysseus's justifications for cheating on his wife is that he never "in his heart" gave consent. In the world of the *Odyssey*, then, there are different types of loyalty (and accordingly many types of infidelity), ranging from physical to emotional.

Questions About Loyalty

1. Can Odysseus be justified in sleeping with Circe and Kalypso?
2. Many of Odysseus's Ithakan friends and subjects believe he is dead, yet he still considers them loyal to him. On the other hand, when Odysseus is killing the suitors, he mentions that they didn't think he was coming back. Home important is faith (so to speak) in

Odysseus's eventual homecoming as a factor in loyalty to him?

Chew on Loyalty

Penelope suffers more for her love of Odysseus than he does for love of her. Telemachos's love for propriety and honor overrides his loyalty to his mother.

Theme of Perseverance

Only through its hero's nearly super-human determination is the *Odyssey* able to reach its glorious conclusion. Odysseus displays over and over his ability to grit his teeth and persevere – over nearly twenty years of hardship. Determination is a virtue in all the major, admirable characters in the epic and takes form in different ways, from physical endurance to emotional steadfastness.

Questions About Perseverance

1. Which is a more vital skill for Odysseus on his journey home – his cunning or his determination?
2. Odysseus is declared god-like in his ability to persevere. How is it that he possesses such "iron" determination? What is it about him and his experiences that might give him greater perseverance than other men?
3. Does Odysseus ever waver in his determination to return home?
4. How does Penelope endure at home in Ithaka? How are her tactics of persevering different from Odysseus's?

Chew on Perseverance

Despite the obvious focus on Odysseus as the ultimate embodiment of perseverance, Penelope deserves this title more than her husband.

Although Odysseus endures many trials at sea, Penelope showed greater perseverance through her endless waiting, consistent belief through her suffering, and dogged determination to hold off her suitors

Theme of Family

The Greek concept of the family reflected in the *Odyssey* includes not only immediate family but ancestors as well. It is oriented toward the past, as men are introduced with their lineage and judged for their name. Still, there are less formal and more emotional aspects to family in this epic; loyalty to one's blood is unwavering, whether it be a wife's faithfulness to her husband, a son's love for his father, or a man's ceaseless determination to get home to his family.

Questions About Family

1. How do sons view their fathers in the *Odyssey*? What characteristics do they wish to emulate?
2. As we all noticed, Homer sometimes gives ancestry and family background for even the most minor of characters. Sure, we might roll our eyes at the seemingly unnecessary digressions, but what might be the point of all this? Why is family history so important to understanding a character in the *Odyssey*?
3. How is the institution of marriage honored in the *Odyssey*, both by the main characters and by minor ones?
4. Are the loyal servants in Odysseus's household considered part of the family? Or is a servant just a servant?

Chew on Family

The father-son relationship is more important to the *Odyssey* that the husband-wife relationship.

The husband-wife relationship is more important to the *Odyssey* than the father-son relationship.

Fate and Free Will Quotes

(Zeus): 'Oh for shame, how the mortals put the blame on us gods, for they say evils come from us, but it is they, rather, who by their own recklessness win sorrow beyond what is given […].' (1.32-34)

Thought: Zeus contends that man does have some control over his own destiny – but does the *Odyssey* argue for or against this point?

(Zeus:) "For his sake Poseidon, shaker of the earth, although he does not kill Odysseus, yet drives him back from the land of his fathers. But come, let all of us who are here work out his homecoming and see to it that he returns. Poseidon shall put away his anger; for all alone and against the will of the other immortal gods united he can accomplish nothing." (1.74-79)

Thought: The way that Poseidon functions under Zeus's will is a perfect example of fate and free will combined. While he must eventually allow Odysseus to go home, he gets to choose how long it takes and how much the man will suffer in the process. Similarly, Odysseus is fated 1) to suffer and 2) to eventually go home, but his actions along the way are a matter of choice. The question then is whether, with the end point decided, the path to get there matters at all.

(Telemachos:) 'My guest, since indeed you are asking me all these questions, there was a time this house was one that might be prosperous and above reproach, when a certain man was here in his country.' (1.231-233)

Thought: Telemachos considers his bad luck the work of the gods. He feels that the gods who favored them so have vanished along with Odysseus. Being abandoned by the gods is, to the ancient Greeks, akin to being cursed.

(Halitherses): 'I who foretell this am not untried, I know what I am saying. Concerning him, I say that everything was accomplished in the way I said it would be at the time the Argives took ship for Ilion, and with them went resourceful Odysseus. I said that after much suffering, with all his companions lost, in the twentieth year, not recognized by any, he would come home. And now all this is being accomplished.' (2.170-176)

Thought: Halitherses will prove the gods' mouthpiece, as many prophets do, by foretelling fate. However, like many prophets, he is ignored and laughed off by the vast ignorant majority.

(Nestor:) 'The will of the everlasting gods is not turned suddenly.' (3.147)

Thought: Nestor disparages Agamemnon for trying to change the will of the gods. Rather than see his additional sacrificing as pious, he accuses the king of trying to change fate. Even better, Nestor says this in the presence of Athene, whose will Agamemnon tried (and failed) to change.

(Nestor:) 'Never once did the wind fail, once the god had set it blowing.' (3.182-183)

Thought: Nestor credits Menelaos's safe journey home to the will of the Gods.

(Menelaos:) '[…] no one of the Achaians labored as much as Odysseus labored and achieved, and for him the end was grief for him, and for me a sorrow that is never forgotten for his sake, how he is gone so long, and we know nothing of whether he is alive or dead.' (4.106-110)

Thought: Menelaos seems to use fate for purposes of comfort; he is able to resign himself and accept his suffering (with regards to his missing friend) because it is the will of the gods.

(Proteus, in Menelaos's tale:) '"But for you, Menelaos, O fostered of Zeus, it is not the gods' will that you shall die and go to your end in horse-pasturing Argos, but the immortals will convey you to the Elysian Field, and the limits of the earth, where fair-haired Rhadamanthys is, and where there is made the easiest life for mortals, for there is no snow, nor much winter there, nor is there ever rain, but always the stream of Ocean sends up breezes of the West Wind blowing briskly for the refreshment of mortals."' (4.561-568)

Thought: The god Proteus tells Menelaos that he is destined for what was a heavenly afterlife to the Greeks – Elysion. Again, Menelaos can find comfort in fate, where others have found only misery.

(Zeus:) '[Odysseus] shall come back by the convoy neither of the gods nor of mortal people, but he shall sail on a jointed raft and, suffering hardships, on the twentieth day make his landfall on fertile Scheria at the country of the Phaiakians who are near the gods in origin, and they will honor him in their hearts as a god, and send him back, by ship, to the beloved land of his fathers, bestowing bronze and hold in abundance upon him, and clothing, more than Odysseus could ever have taken away from Troy, even if he had escaped unharmed with his fair share of the plunder. For so it is fated that he shall see his people and come back to his house with the high roof and to the land of his fathers.' (5.31-42)

Thought: Zeus reveals that it is his will – and thus Fate – that Odysseus should reach Ithaka safely and with treasure – but without his friends at his side. Fate, then, is determined by the will of this god and subject to change at his whim; it isn't a pre-planned determination.

(Ino:) 'Poor man, why is Poseidon the shaker of the earth so bitterly cankered against you, to give you such a harvest of evils? And yet he will not do away with you, for all his anger. But do as I say, since you seem to me not lacking in good sense. Take off these clothes, and leave the raft to drift at the winds' will, and then strike out and swim with your hands and make for a landfall on the Phaiakian country, where your escape is destined.' (5.339-344)

Thought: Apparently, Odysseus's fate is common knowledge – even among the lesser gods.

(Odysseus, in his tale:) "We are Achaians coming from Troy, beaten off our true course by winds from every direction across the great gulf of the open sea, making for home, by the wrong way, on the wrong courses. So we have come. So it has pleased Zeus to arrange it."' (9.259-262)

Thought: Here Odysseus tries to win sympathy from Polyphemos, the Cyclops, by pointing out that it wasn't his fault that he came to his shore.

(Odysseus:) 'Next I told the rest of the men to cast lots, to find out which of them must endure with me to take up the great beam and spin it in the Cyclops' eye when sweet sleep had come over him. The ones drew it whom I myself would have wanted chosen, four men, and I myself was the fifth, and allotted with them.' (9.331-335)

Thought: Questions of fate and luck pervade the *Odyssey* – even in the smallest of instances.

(Polyphemos, in Odysseus's tale:) *"'Hear me, Poseidon who circle the earth, dark-haired. If truly I am your son, and you acknowledge yourself as my father, grant that Odysseus, sacker of cities, son of Laertes, who makes his home in Ithaka, may never reach that home; but if it is decided that he shall see his own people, and come home to his strong-founded house and to his own country, let him come late, in bad case, with the loss of all his companions, in someone else's ship, and find troubles in his household." 'So he spoke in prayer, and the dark-haired god heard him.'* (9.528-536)

Thought: Wounded Polyphemos invokes his father Poseidon as well as Fate to his aid in cursing Odysseus. This is excellent evidence that notions of fate and free will are not mutually exclusive. Odysseus chooses to blind the Cyclops and to reveal his name, *therefore* it is his fate to suffer at sea. His pride, not his destiny, determines the following course of events.

(Circe, in Odysseus's tale:) *"'Son of Laertes and seed of Zeus, resourceful Odysseus, you shall no longer stay in my house when none of you wish to; but first there is another journey you must accomplish and reach the house of Hades and of revered Persephone, there to consult with the soul of Teiresias the Theban, the blind prophet, whose senses stay unshaken within him, to whom alone Persephone has granted intelligence even after death, but the rest of them are flittering shadows.'"* (10.488-495)

Thought: It might seem kind of weird how Circe just suddenly up and tells Odysseus that he has to go to the Underworld, though since she's a (minor) goddess herself, it kind of makes sense that she would know the will of the gods. Anyway, it's important to remember that this comes from the part of the story narrated by Odysseus himself, in which we never get a "behind-the-scenes" look at what the gods are planning. Like Odysseus, we're just along for the ride in this part of the story.

(Elpenor, in Odysseus's tale:) *"'Son of Laertes and seed of Zeus, resourceful Odysseus, the evil will of the spirit and the wild wine bewildered me. I lay down on the roof of Circe's palace, and never thought, when I went down, to go by way of the long ladder, but blundered straight off the edge of the roof, so that my neck bone was broken out of its sockets, and my soul went down to Hades'. […] I know that after you leave this place and the house of Hades you will put back with your well-made ship to the island, Aiaia; there at that time, my lord, I ask that you remember me, and do not go and leave me behind unwept, unburied, when he leave, for fear I might become the gods' curse upon you; but burn me there with all my armor that belongs to me, and heap up a grave mound beside the beach of that gray sea, for an unhappy man, so that those to come will know of me. Do this for me, and on top of the grave mound plant the oar with which I rowed when I was alive and among my companions.'"* (11.60-65, 69-78)

Thought: We wish every drunken mistake we make could be chalked up to luck or fate. Oh, and if you wanted, you could read Elpenor's fate as a test for Odysseus, a test of his own piety and, in turn, whether or not he is worthy of his own destiny.

(Teiresias, in Odysseus's tale:) "'Glorious Odysseus, what you are after is sweet homecoming, but the god will make it hard for you. I think you will not escape Shaker of the Earth, who holds a grudge against you in his heart, and because you blinded his dear son, hates you. But even so and still you might come back, after much suffering, if you can contain your own desire, and contain your companions'[...].'" (11.100-105)

Thought: Teiresias prophecies much suffering, but gives a rather nuanced vision of fate. He implies that Odysseus might indeed die – despite all the favoritism shown him by Athene – if he does not discipline himself and his shipmates. Odysseus's goal, Teiresias suggests, may only be reached if Odysseus follows his advice. So if you're at all interested in the fate vs. free will argument in the *Odyssey*, bookmark the heck out of this page in your book. You're going to have to address this passage in one way or another.

(Odysseus, in his tale:) "'Aias, son of stately Telamon, could you then never even in death forget your anger against me, because of that cursed armor? The gods made it to pain the Achaians, so great a bulwark were you, who were lost to them. We Achaians grieved for your death as incessantly as for Achilleus the son of Peleus at his death, and there is no other to blame, but Zeus; he, in his terrible hate for the army of the Danaan spearmen, visited this destruction upon you.'" (11.553-560)

Thought: Odysseus tries to reclaim Aias's friendship by reminding him that his death was purely ill-starred and no fault of his. He blames Zeus, and not Aias, for taking his life and reminds his friend that one cannot always control his own fate.

(Odysseus:) 'My men were thrown in the water, and bobbing like sea crows they were washed away on the running waves all around the black ship, and the god took away their homecoming.' (12.417-419)

Thought: Zeus's destruction of Odysseus's ship is fated once the men kill Helios's cattle. This again shows that men can influence or indeed determine their fates. They made the conscious choice to kill the sacred cattle, and now they must pay the price, right? On the other hand, couldn't it have been fated for them to make that choice? This is one of those classic free-will brainteasers.

(Alkinoös:) 'Ah now, the prophecy of old is come to completion, that my father spoke, when he said Poseidon someday would be angry with us, because we are convoy without hurt to all men. He said that one day, as a well-made ship of Phaiakian men came back from a convoy on the misty face of the water, he would stun it, and pile a great mountain on our city, to hide it.' (13.172-177)

Thought: Alkinoös interprets this sign as a fulfillment of the prophecy his father read. Do you think the Phaiakians could have done anything to avoid their fate?

(Theoklymenos:) 'Telemachos, not without a god's will did this bird fly past you on the right, for I knew when I saw it that it was a portent. No other family shall be kinglier than yours in the country of Ithaka, but you shall have lordly power forever.' (15.531-534)

Thought: Good to know. But prophets in the *Odyssey* tend to throw out these sorts of statements without providing the necessary conditions. That's what makes Odysseus's conversation with Teiresias so unique.

[Amphinomos] went back across the room, heart saddened within him, shaking his head, for in his spirit he saw the evil, but still could not escape his doom, for Athene had bound him fast, to be strongly killed by the hands and spear of Telemachos. (18.153-156)

Thought: Amphinomos, in a rare epiphany, realizes that what he has done as a suitor will bring death upon him. Is the fact that Homer tells us ahead of time of his death by Telemachos's spear a nod to some form of pre-determination?

'Poor wretches, what evil has come on you? Your heads and faces and the knees underneath you are shrouded in night and darkness; a sound of wailing has broken out, your cheeks are covered with tears, and the walls bleed, and the fine supporting pillars. All the forecourt is huddled with ghosts, the yard is full of them as they flock down to the underworld and the darkness. The sun has perished out of the sky, and a foul mist has come over.' So he spoke, and all of them laughed happily at him. (20.351-358)

Thought: The seer predicts damnation and darkness for the suitors for their treachery. He turns out, like most seers, to be right. What the heck is the rest of the suitors' problem? We definitely wouldn't be laughing in their place!

[Antinoös] was to be the first to get a taste of the arrow from the hands of blameless Odysseus, to whom he now paid attention as he sat in Odysseus' halls and encouraged all his companions. (21.98-100)

Thought: The poet shows us the gods' intention for Antinoös – he will be the first to die at Odysseus's hand for his insolence. Do his actions determine his fate?

And now Athene waved the aegis, that blights humanity, from high aloft on the roof, and all their wits were bewildered; and they stampeded about the hall, like a herd of cattle set upon and driven wild by the darting horse fly [...]. (22.297-300)

Thought: Athene finally reveals what we all already know: that she will fight by Odysseus's side. This was destined to happen and the sign bound to show, so the only question was when. Certain events, we see, are predetermined, but the execution and timing of those events are left to choice.

Then standing close beside him gray-eyed Athene said to him: 'Son of Arkeisios, far dearest of all my companions, make your prayer to the gray-eyed girl and to Zeus her father, then quickly balance your far-shadowing spear, and throw it.' So Pallas Athene spoke, and breathed into him enormous strength, and, making his prayer then to the daughter of Zeus, he quickly balanced his far-shadowing spear, and threw it, and struck Eupeithes on the brazen side of his helmet, nor could the helm hold off the spear, but the bronze smashed clean through. (24.516-524)

Thought: Telemachos's invocation powers his spear straight through Eupeithes's helmet –he made the decision to hurl the spear, but the will of a god rendered the throw fatal.

Piety Quotes

(Eurymachos:) '[…] in any case we fear no one, and surely not Telemachos, for all he is so eloquent. Nor do we care for any prophecy, which you, old sir, may tell us, which will not happen, and will make you even more hated.'

Thought: Eurymachos and the suitors disrespect the gods by dismissing Telemachos, who is favored by Athene, and Halitherses, who speaks the gods' will. By laughing off the words of those through whom the gods speak, they are placing themselves in opposition to divine law. So they will be punished.

When they had made fast the running gear all along the black ship, then they set up the mixing bowls, filling them brimful with wine, and poured to the gods immortal and everlasting but beyond all other gods they poured to Zeus' gray-eyed daughter. (2.430-433)

Thought: Telemachos's men show their piety by making the proper libations to the gods, especially to Athene – though they do not know she is helping them.

They came to Pylos, Neleus' strong-founded citadel, where the people on the shore of the sea were making sacrifice of bulls who were all black to the dark-haired Earthshaker. There were nine settlements of them, and in each five hundred holdings, and from each of these nine bulls were provided. (3.4-8)

Thought: The residents show their piety by holding ritual sacrifices to their patron god, Poseidon. Their piety implicitly renders Nestor, ruler of this land, a trustworthy friend for Telemachos.

Then in turn the gray-eyed goddess Athene answered him: 'Telemachos, some of it you yourself will see in your own heart, and some the divinity will put in your mind. I do not think you could have been born and reared without the gods' will.' (3.25-28)

Thought: Athene tells Telemachos to have faith in himself and in the gods since they have always favored him. She herself, loving Telemachos for Odysseus's sake, gives him the words and courage to speak eloquently to Nestor.

(Athene:) 'Hear us, Poseidon, who circle the earth, and do not begrudge us the accomplishment of all these actions for which we pray you. First of all to Nestor and to his sons grant glory, and then on all the rest of the Pylians besides confer gracious recompense in return for this grand hecatomb, and yet again grant that Telemachos and I go back with that business done for which we came this way in our black ship.' (3.55-61)

Thought: This is ironic, as one disguised goddess asks only nominally for another's help. Athene, disguised as Mentor, invokes Poseidon to maintain her disguise, but really doesn't need his help. In fact she grants every one of her wishes herself.

(Nestor:) 'Act quickly now, dear children, and do me this favor, so that I may propitiate first of all the gods, Athene, who came plainly to me at our happy feasting in the god's honor. Come then, let one man go to the field for a cow, so that she may come with all speed, and let one of the oxherds be driving her, and one go down to the black ship of great-hearted Telemachos, and bring back all his companions, leaving only two beside her, and yet another go tell the worker in gold Laerkes to come, so that he can cover the cow's horns with gold. You others stay here all together in a group but tell the serving women who are in the house to prepare a glorious dinner, and set chairs and firewood in readiness, and fetch bright water.' (3.418-429)

Thought: Nestor combines piety with hospitality – because proper hosting is the mandate of Zeus, these two virtues are rightfully intertwined.

(Proteus, in Menelaos's tale:) '"But you should have made grand sacrifices to Zeus and the other immortal gods, and so gone on board, so most quickly to reach your own country, sailing over the wine-blue water. It is not your destiny now to see your own people and come back to your strong-founded house and to the land of your fathers, until you have gone back once again to the water of Egypt, the sky-fallen river, and there have accomplished holy hecatombs in honor of all the immortal gods who hold wide heaven. Then the gods will grant you that journey that you so long for."' (4.472-480)

Thought: Looks like sacrifice really can solve all your problems. Unless your name is Agamemnon.

'[…] and Aias would have escaped his doom, though Athene hated him, had he not gone wildly mad and tossed out a word of defiance; for he said that in despite of the gods he escaped the great gulf of the sea, and Poseidon heard him, loudly vaunting, and at once with his ponderous hands catching up the trident he drove it against the Gyrean rock, and split a piece off it, and part of it stayed where it was, but a splinter crashed in the water, and this was where Aias had been perched when he raved so madly. It carried him down to the depths of the endless and tossing main sea. So Aias died, when he had swallowed down the salt water.' (4.502-511)

Thought: Aias is killed simply for his impiety. This serves as a warning for Odysseus not to let his pride get out of hand.

(Odysseus:) 'Hear me, my lord, whoever you are. I come in great need to you, a fugitive from the sea and the curse of Poseidon; even for immortal gods that man has a claim on their mercy who comes to them as a wandering man, in the way that I now come to your current and to your knees after much suffering. Pity me then, my lord. I call myself your supplicant.' He spoke, and the river stayed its current, stopped the waves breaking, and made all quiet in front of him and let him get safely into the outlet of the river.' (5.445-454)

Thought: Odysseus's piety in his prayer to the river god saves his life.

(Polyphemos, in Odysseus's tale:) '"Stranger, you are a simple fool, or come from far off, when you tell me to avoid the wrath of the gods or fear them. The Cyclopes do not concern themselves over Zeus of the aegis, nor any of the rest of the blessed gods, since we are far better than they […]."' (9.273-287)

Thought: Polyphemos offends the gods by snubbing their will for hosts to treat their guests well. But he goes so far as to say that he does not mind the gods' decrees at all and, furthermore, has no fear of them. Impiety at its finest, but Polyphemos seems to be exempt from the consequences, maybe because he's the son of a god, maybe because his world (and therefore rules, customs, and traditions) is made separate from the rest of the world by its isolation.

(Odysseus:) '[…] for me alone my strong-greaved companions excepted the ram when the sheep were sheared, and I sacrificed him on the sands to Zeus, dark-clouded son of Kronos, lord over all, and burned him the thighs; but he was not moved by my offerings, but still was pondering on a way how all my strong-benched ships should be destroyed and all my eager companions.' (9.550-555)

Thought: OK, so sacrifices aren't exactly a get-out-of-jail-free card – not when you've committed as grave an impiety as Odysseus has (harming the son of a major god and then bragging about it).

(Teiresias, in Odysseus's tale:) "'But after you have killed these suitors in your palace, either by treachery, or openly with the sharp bronze, then you must take up your well-shaped oar and go on a journey until you come where there are men living who know nothing of the sea, and who eat food that is not mixed with salt, who never have known ships whose cheeks are painted purple, who never have known-well-shaped oars, which act for ships as wings do. And I will tell you a very clear proof, and you cannot miss it. When, as you walk, some other wayfarer happens to meet you, and says you carry a winnow-fan on your bright shoulder, then you must plant your well-shaped oar in the ground, and render ceremonious sacrifice to the lord Poseidon, one ram and one bull, and a mounter of sows, a boar pig, and make your way home again and render holy hecatombs to the immortal gods who hold the wide heaven, all of them in order. Death will come to you from the sea, in some altogether unwarlike way, and it will end you in the ebbing time of a sleek old age. Your people about you will be prosperous. All this is true that I tell you.'" (11.119-137)

Thought: Here, Teiresias tells Odysseus about his ultimate fate – which will happen after the end of the *Odyssey*. How does this knowledge of Odysseus's eventual death affect the mood at the end of the poem?

(Odysseus:) 'Then I went away along the island in order to pray to the gods, if any of them might show me some course to sail on, but when, crossing the isle, I had left my companions behind, I washed my hands, where there was a place sheltered from the wind, and prayed to all the gods whose hold is Olympos; but what they did was to shed a sweet sleep on my eyelids […].' (12.333-338)

Thought: Then again…

(Odysseus:) 'You dogs, you never thought I would any more come back from the land of Troy, and because of that you despoiled my household, and forcibly took my serving women to sleep beside you, and sought to win my wife while I was still alive, fearing neither the immortal gods who hold the wide heaven, nor any resentment sprung from men to be yours in the future. Now upon you all the terms of destruction are fastened.' (22.35-41)

Thought: Odysseus cites the suitors' crime as one not only of incivility, but of impiety as well.

(Odysseus:) 'Keep your joy in your heart, old dame; stop, do not raise up the cry. It is not piety to glory so over slain men. These were destroyed by the doom of the gods and their own hard actions […].' (22.411-413)

Thought: We learn that it is impious to rejoice at the death of others, even if those others were jerks that totally got what was coming to them. Compare this older, wiser Odysseus to the man who taunted Polyphemos from his departing ship.

Justice Quotes

(Telemachos:) '[…] fear also the gods' anger, lest they, astonished by evil actions, turn against you. I supplicate you, by Zeus the Olympian and by Themis who breaks up the assemblies of men and calls them in session: let be, my friends, and leave me alone with my bitter sorrow to waste away; unless my noble father Odysseus at some time in anger did evil to the strong-greaved Achaians, for which angry with me in revenge you do me evil in setting these on me.' (2.66-74)

Thought: Telemachos, despite his youth, has a clear understanding of the way justice works: if one is god-fearing and shows it through the proper behavior, he will be rewarded. The suitors, in dishonoring the house of Odysseus, are also dishonoring the gods, and risk having the gods turn against them.

(Telemachos:) 'Antinoös, I cannot thrust the mother who bore me, who raised me, out of the house against her will. My father, alive or dead, is elsewhere in the world. It will be hard to pay back Ikarios, if willingly I dismiss my mother. I will suffer some evil from her father, and the spirit will give me more yet, for my mother will call down her furies upon me as she goes out of the house, and I shall have the people's resentment.' (2.130-137)

Thought: Telemachos's refusal to banish his mother is accompanied not by a rash or emotional response, but rather by a logical reasoning grounded in his understanding of justice. The Prince's later claim that he is not trained in public speaking seems unnecessarily humble.

(Polyphemos, in Odysseus's tale:) '"Hear me, Poseidon, who circle the earth, dark-haired. If truly I am your son, and you acknowledge yourself as my father, grant that Odysseus, sacker of cities, son of Laertes, who makes his home in Ithaka, may never reach that home; but if it is decided that he shall see his own people, and come home to his strong-founded house and to his own country, let him come late, in bad case, with the loss of all his companions, in someone else's ship, and find troubles in his household." 'So he spoke in prayer, and the dark-haired god heard him.' (9.528-536)

Thought: Wounded Polyphemos believes that he is asking merely for justice. True, Odysseus wounded him, but not before Polyphemos violated Zeus's laws of hospitality. Whether or not Odysseus's prolonged suffering is "just" is up for debate.

(Helios, in Odysseus's tale:) '"Father Zeus, and you other everlasting and blessed gods, punish the companions of Odysseus, son of Laertes; for they outrageously killed my cattle, in whom I always delighted, on my way up into the starry heaven, or when I turned back again from heaven toward earth. Unless these are made to give me just recompense for my cattle, I will go down to Hades' and give my light to dead men."' (12.377-383)

Thought: Odysseus's men were repeatedly warned not to touch the sacred cattle; does this mean their deaths are just?

(Alkinoös:) '[…] let us man by man each one of us give a great tripod and a caldron, and we will make it good to us by a collection among the people. It is hard for a single man to be generous.' (13.13-15)

Thought: Alkinoös believes that repaying Odysseus for all that he has lost – his men, twenty years of his life – is only justice for the poor man's suffering.

(Athene:) 'It is true that the young men with their black ship are lying in wait for him to kill him before he reaches his country; but I think this will not happen, but that sooner the earth will cover some one of those suitors, who now are eating away your substance.' (13.425-428)

Thought: Athene reminds us that the suitors deserve death not only for violating the laws of hospitality, but for plotting to kill Telemachos.

[Antinoös] was to be the first to get a taste of the arrow from the hands of blameless Odysseus, to whom he now paid attention as he sat in Odysseus' halls and encouraged all his companions. (21.98-100)

Thought: That Antinoös dies first is a just punishment for his actions.

(Odysseus:) 'You dogs, you never thought I would any more come back from the land of Troy, and because of that you despoiled my household, and forcibly took my serving women to sleep beside you, and sought to win my wife while I was still alive, fearing neither the immortal gods who hold the wide heaven, nor any resentment sprung from men to be yours in the future. Now upon you all the terms of destruction are fastened.' […] [A]ll that you have now, and what you could add from elsewhere, even so, I would not stay my hands from the slaughter, until I had taken revenge for all the suitors' transgression. Now the choice has been set before you, either to fight me or run, if any of you can escape death and its spirits. But I think not one man will escape from sheer destruction.' (22.35-41, 62-67)

Thought: Odysseus, like his son earlier, doesn't use his emotion or anger to explain his actions. Instead, he rationalizes them with the laws of justice.

(Odysseus:) 'O son of Polytherses, lover of mockery, never speak loud and all at random in your recklessness. Rather leave all speech to the gods, since they are far stronger than you are. Here is your guest gift, in exchange for that hoof you formerly gave to godlike Odysseus, as he went about through the palace.' (22.287-291)

Thought: Is it justice that Ktesippos receives death for throwing a cow's foot at a beggar?

(Odysseus:) 'Keep your joy in your heart, old dame; stop, do not raise up the cry. It is not piety to glory so over slain men. These were destroyed by the doom of the gods and their own hard actions [...].' (22.411-413)

Thought: Odysseus reminds Eurykleia that the suitors were not killed for personal pleasure (therefore, they should not rejoice at the fallen men). Rather, the men had to be killed for reasons of justice.

(Athene:) 'Hold back, men of Ithaka, from the wearisome fighting, so that most soon, and without blood, you can settle everything.' (24.531-532)

Thought: Athene maintains that justice need not always be served at the end of a sword.

Pride Quotes

(Nestor:) 'If only gray-eyed Athene would deign to love you, as in those days she used so to take care of glorious Odysseus in the Trojan country, where we Achaians suffered miseries; for I never saw the gods showing such open affection as Pallas Athene, the way she stood beside him, openly; if she would deign to love you as she did him, and care for you in her heart, then some of those people might well forget about marrying.' Then the thoughtful Telemachos said to him in answer: 'Old sir, I think that what you have said will not be accomplished. What you mean is too big. It bewilders me. That which I hope for could never happen to me, not even if the gods so willed it.' (3.218-288)

Thought: Is Telemachos showing humility here? Or are his words just another form of pride—believing his own problems are so big that even the gods couldn't fix them?

(Telemachos:) 'The court of Zeus must be like this on the inside, such abundance of everything. Wonder takes me as I look on it.' Menelaos of the fair hair overheard him speaking, and now he spoke to both of them and addressed them in winged words: 'Dear children, there is no mortal who could rival Zeus, seeing that his mansions are immortal and his possessions.' (4.74-79)

Thought: When Telemachos remarks that Menelaos's court is godly, Menelaos shows his humility by saying that no mortal man can rival the splendor of the gods.

Now Peisistratos son of Nestor spoke up before him: 'Great Menelaos, son of Atreus, leader of the people, this in in truth the son of that man, just as you are saying; but he is modest, and his spirit would be shocked at the thought of coming here and beginning a show of reckless language in front of you, for we both delight in your voice [...].' (4.155-160)

Thought: Telemachos is so shy and humble that Peisistratos must speak up to recognize him as Odysseus's son. Telemachos will not claim such an illustrious heritage himself. Peisistratos makes it known that Telemachos has a graceful humility about him and does not go looking for attention for his glorious bloodline.

(Menelaos:) '[…] and Aias would have escaped his doom, though Athene hated him, had he not gone wildly mad and tossed out a word of defiance; for he said that in despite of the gods he escaped the great gulf of the sea, and Poseidon heard him, loudly vaunting, and at once with his ponderous hands catching up the trident he drove it against the Gyrean rock, and split a piece off it, and part of it stayed where it was, but a splinter crashed in the water, and this was where Aias had been perched when he raved so madly. It carried him down to the depths of the endless and tossing main sea. So Aias died, when he had swallowed down the salt water.' (4.502-511)

Thought: Aias's story can be seen as a warning to Odysseus not to let his own pride get out of hand, lest he anger the gods with his hubris.

(Alkinoös:) 'Now let us go outside and make our endeavor in all contests, so that our stranger can tell his friends, after he reaches his home, by how much we surpass all others in boxing, wrestling, leaping and speed of our feet for running.' (8.100-103)

Thought: Alkinoös's pride in his people and their reputation is evident here, but it is not an unwarranted. Pride, then, isn't inherently harmful in the *Odyssey*: Homer draws a distinction between healthy pride and hubris.

(Odysseus:) 'I know well how to handle the polished bow, and would be first to strike any man with an arrow aimed at a company of hostile men, even though many companions were standing close beside me, and all shooting with bows at the enemies. There was Philoktetes alone who surpassed me in archery when we Achaians shot with bows in the Trojan country. But I will say that I stand far out ahead of all others such as are living mortals now and feed on the earth. Only I will not set myself against men of the generations before, not with Herakles nor Eurytos of Oichalia, who set themselves against the immortals with the bow, and therefore great Eurytos died suddenly nor came to an old age in his own mansions, since Apollo in anger against him killed him, because he had challenged Apollo in archery.' (8.215-228)

Thought: Odysseus's speaks highly of his own abilities; that said, he is careful not to compare himself to guys from past generations. Those guys went too far in their pride and crossed over into hubris. If you do that, you risk coming to a bad end—like that Eurytos dude Odysseus is talking about.

(Odysseus, in his tale:) 'Cyclops, in the end it was no weak man's companions you were to eat by violence and force in your hollow cave, and your evil deeds were to catch up with you, and be too strong for you, hard one, who dared to eat your own guests in your own house, so Zeus and the rest of the gods have punished you.' (9.475-479)

Thought: Translation: "How do you like me *now*?"

(Odysseus:) 'So they spoke, but could not persuade the great heart in me, but once again in the anger of my heart I cried to him: "Cyclops, if any mortal man ever asks you who it was that inflicted upon your eye this shameful blinding, tell him that you were blinded by Odysseus, sacker of cities. Laertes is his father, and he makes his home on Ithaka." (9.500-505)

Thought: Why does Odysseus mock the Cyclops? It seems again to be a matter of pride over his genius; he wants the world to know that he, Odysseus, was the man to best the monster. Quite cleverly, too, if he does say so himself.

(Odysseus:) 'Nevertheless we sailed on, night and day, for nine days, and on the tenth at last appeared the land of our fathers, and we could see people tending fires, we were very close to them. But then the sweet sleep came upon me, for I was worn out with always handling the sheet myself, and I could not give it to any other companion, so we could come home quicker to our own country; but my companions talked with each other and said that I was bringing silver and gold home with me, given me by great-hearted Aiolos, son of Hippotas; […] and the evil counsel of my companions prevailed, and they opened the bag and the winds all burst out. Suddenly the storm caught them away and swept them over the water weeping, away from their own country.' (10.28-36, 46-49)

Thought: Could Odysseus's pride be the culprit here? If he had told his men what was in the bag rather than lording it over them, they never would have opened the sack. On the other hand, his men's sense of pride is responsible too—because they are too high-and-mighty to just put up with what their captain tells them.

(Odysseus, in his tale:) 'Aias, son of stately Telamon, could you then never even in death forget your anger against me, because of that cursed armor? The gods made it to pain the Achaians, so great a bulwark were you, who were lost to them. We Achaians grieved for your death as incessantly as for Achilleus the son of Peleus at his death, and there is no other to blame, but Zeus; he, in his terrible hate for the army of Danaan spearmen, visited this destruction upon you. Come nearer, my lord, so you can hear what I say and listen to my story; suppress your anger and lordly spirit.' (11.553-562)

Thought: Odysseus considers Aias's death to be a sign of his excessive pride. The story behind the death happened in Troy, when Odysseus and Aias competed for the arms of Achilleus, who had been killed. The arms were to go to the bravest man and the Greeks could not decide between the two, for fear of losing one in the war effort. So they let the captive Trojans decide and Odysseus won. Enraged, Aias killed himself. Now, Odysseus swallows his

own pride to try to make amends with Aias; he asks Aias to do the same.

(Odysseus, in his tale:) "Come then, goddess, answer me truthfully this: is there some way for me to escape away from deadly Charybdis, but yet fight the other off, when she attacks my companions?" 'So I spoke, and she, shining among goddesses, answered: "Hardy man, your mind is full forever of fighting and battle work. Will you not give way even to the immortals? She is no mortal thing byt a mischief immortal, dangerous, difficult and bloodthirsty, and there is no fighting against her, nor any force of defense. It is best to run away from her." (12.112-120)

Thought: Odysseus shows pride in trying to fight off fate; he thinks he can shrug off the will of the gods by simple display of mortal strength.

[Melanthios] recklessly lashed out with his heel to the hip, but failed to knock him out of the pathway, for Odysseus stood it, unshaken, while he pondered within him whether to go for him with his cudgel, and take the life from him or pick him up like a jug and break his head on the ground. Yet still he stood it, and kept it all inside him. (17.233-238)

Thought: Odysseus controls his raging dignity. He takes offense at being touched so offensively by a lonely goatherd, but reins in his pride long enough to keep his crucial secret.

(Odysseus:) 'Leave blows alone, do not press me too hard, or you may make me angry so that, old as I am, I may give you a bloody chest and mouth. Then I could have peace, and still more of it tomorrow, for I do not think you will make your way back here a second time to the house of Odysseus, son of Laertes.' (18.20-24)

Thought: Still, Odysseus can't hold out in the land of humility forever. He flaunts his old glory as a warrior, even though it risks foiling his beggar disguise.

(Penelope:) 'Eurymachos, all my excellence, my beauty and figure, were ruined by the immortals at that time when the Argives took ship for Ilion, and with them went my husband, Odysseus. If he were to come back to me and take care of my life, then my reputation would be more great and splendid.' (18.251-255)

Thought: Penelope considers her as beauty lost with Odysseus's departure. This is particularly humble of her, since Athene has just given her a super-special goddess makeover.

(Antinoös:) 'Ah, wretched stranger, you have no sense, not even a little. Is it not enough that you dine in peace, among us, who are violent men, and are deprived of no fair portion, but listen to our conversation and what we say? But thereis no other vagabond and newcomer who is allowed to hear us talk. The honeyed wine has hurt you, as it has distracted others as well, who gulp it down without drinking in season.' (21.288-294)

Thought: Antinoös obviously esteems himself above the beggar and sees the man as unfit for the table. Ironically, the true identity of the beggar far outranks him, and Antinoös is actually unjustified. Additionally, Antinoös has been repeatedly berated for looking like a nobleman but acting like a tramp. Both in his case and the case of the beggar, appearances are deceiving.

Lies and Deceit Quotes

[Athene] caught up a powerful spear, edged with sharp bronze, heavy, huge, thick, wherewith she beats down the battalions of fighting men, against whom she of the mighty father is angered, and descended in a flash of speed from the peaks of Olympos, and lighted in the land of Ithaka, at the doors of Odysseus at the threshold of the court, and in her hand was the bronze spear. She was disguised as a friend, leader of the Taphians, Mentes. (1.99-105)

Thought: Athene appropriately takes on the guise of Odysseus's friend in order to help Telemachos. The mask fits in this case. Still, there's a quite a contrast between that mask—of some kindly old dude—and her true nature, hopscotching her way down from the home of the gods!

(Telemachos:) 'Eurymachos, there is no more hope of my father's homecoming. I believe no messages any more, even should there be one, nor pay attention to any prophecy, those times my mother calls some diviner into the house and asks him questions.' (1.413-416)

Thought: Athene has just told Telemachos that his father is still alive, but the Prince chooses to deceive the suitors to keep him and his mother safe; it seems he fears a riot or coup if the men all knew the truth.

(Antinoös:) And here is another stratagem of her heart's devising. She set up a great loom in her palace, and set to weaving a web of threads long and fine. Then she said to us: "Young men, my suitors now that the great Odysseus has perished, wait, though you are eager to marry me, until I finish this web, so that my weaving will not be useless and wasted. This is a shroud for the hero Laertes, for when the destructive doom of death which lays men low shall take him, lest any Achaian woman in this neighborhood hold it against me that a man of many conquests lies with no sheet to wind him." So she spoke, and the proud heart in us was persuaded. Thereafter in the daytime she would weave at her great loom, but in the night she would have torches set by, and undo it. So for three years she was secret in her design, convincing the Achaians […]. (2.93-106)

Thought: Penelope can rival her husband in trickery.

So he spoke in prayer, and from nearby Athene came to him likening herself to Mentor in voice and appearance. Now she spoke aloud to him and addressed him in winged words: 'Telemachos, you are to be no thoughtless man, no coward, if truly the strong force of your father is instilled in you; such a man he was for accomplishing word and action.' (2.267-272)

Thought: Athene uses deception, but for the purpose of speaking the truth.

(Telemachos:) 'Do not fear, nurse. This plan was not made without a god's will. But swear to tell my beloved mother nothing about this until the eleventh day has come or the twelfth hereafter, or until she misses me herself or hears I am absent, so that she may not ruin her lovely skin with weeping.' (2.372-376)

Thought: Telemachos's deception extends even to his own mother.

Now Helen, who was descended of Zeus, thought of the next thing. Into the wine of which they were drinking she cast a medicine of heartsease, free of gall, to make one forget all sorrows, and whoever had drunk it down once it had been mixed in the wine bowl, for the day that he drank it would have no tear roll down his face, not if his mother died and his father died, not if men murdered a brother or a beloved son in his presence. (4.219-225)

Thought: Surprisingly, much of the deceit we see in the Odyssey is far from harmful. Often, as in this instance with Helen, it is beneficial; her drug eases the men's pain and replaces their tears with laughter.

(Helen:) 'He flagellated himself with degrading strokes, then threw on a worthless sheet about his shoulders. He looked like a servant. So he crept into the wide-wayed city of the men he was fighting, disguising himself in the likeness of somebody else, a beggar, one who was unlike himself beside the ships of the Achaians, but in his likeness crept into the Trojan's city, and they all were taken in.' (4.244-250)

Thought: Odysseus has built his reputation as a national hero from his ability to deceive.

(Menelaos:) 'Three times you walked around the hollow ambush, feeling it, and you called out, naming them by name, to the best of the Danaans, and made your voice sound like the voice of the wife of each of the Argives. Now I myself and the son of Tydeus and great Odysseus were sitting there in the middle of them and we heard you crying aloud, and Diomedes and I started up, both minded to go outside, or else to answer your voice from inside, but Odysseus pulled us back and held us, for all our eagerness.' (4.277-284)

Thought: It's interesting that Menelaos is able to laugh at this story; remember, it was all for the sake of getting Helen back that the Achaians went to war with the Trojans in the first place. But that's not all that's weird—notice how Helen tricks the Achaians (whom she somehow knows are in the horse) by pretending to sound like their wives. Menelaos himself is fooled; does that mean Helen was pretending to be… herself? Weird. Anyway, with master tricksters, it apparently takes one to know one—notice that it's Odysseus who prevents the other Achaians from letting the cat out of the bag, so to speak.

(Menelaos:) 'Meanwhile she had dived down into the sea's great cavern and brought back the skins of four seals out of the water. All were newly skinned. She was planning a trick on her father. And hollowing out four beds in the sand of the sea, she sat there waiting for us, and we came close up to to her. Thereupon she bedded us down in order, and spread a skin over each man. That was a most awful ambush, for the pernicious smell of those seals, bred in the salt water, oppressed us terribly.' (4.435-442)

Thought: Even gods (in this case, Proteus) are deceived by disguise in the *Odyssey*.

So he [Noëmon] spoke, and they were amazed at heart; they had not thought he had gone to Pylos, the city of Neleus, but that he was somewhere near, on his lands, among the flocks, or else with the swineherd. (4.638-640)

Thought: Telemachos: 1 The suitors: 0

(Penelope:) 'Hear me, dear friends. The Olympian has given me sorrows beyond all others who were born and brought up together with me for first I lost a husband with the heart of a lion and who among the Danaans surpassed in all virtues, and great, whose fame goes wide through Hellas and midmost Argos; and now again the stormwinds have caught away my beloved son, without trace, from the halls, and I never heard when he left me. Hard-hearted, not one out of all of you then remembered to wake me out of my bed, though your minds knew all clearly, when he went out and away to board the hollow black ship. For if I had heard that he was considering this journey, then he would have had to stay, though hastening to his voyage, or he would have had to leave me dead in the halls.' (4.722-735)

Thought: Penelope essentially says she would have let her son sail only over her dead body. She is angered not only by his absence, but by the deception that hid his departure from her. Moms will be moms.

[Athene] drifted in like a breath of wind to where the girl slept, and came and stood above her head and spoke a word to her, likening herself to the daughter of Dymas, famed for seafaring, a girl of the same age, in whom her fancy delighted. (6.20-23)

Thought: Athene manipulates Nausikaa for her own purposes; no one seems to care that the Princess gets the short end of this (she lusts after Odysseus, who isn't really in a position to respond to such desires).

Then Odysseus rose to go to the city. Athene with kind thought for Odysseus drifted a deep mist about him, for fear some one of the great-hearted Phaiakians, meeting him, might speak to him in a sneering way and ask where he came from. But when he was about to enter the lovely city, there the gray-eyed goddess Athene met him, in the likeness of a young girl, a little maid, carrying a pitcher […]. (7.14-20)

Thought: Athene is a master of disguise – cloaking Odysseus from view with her magical fog and simultaneously disguising herself as a little Phaiakian girl. Thus disguises here don't just deceive, but – in Odysseus's case – hide completely from view.

Pallas Athene went through the city, likening herself to the herald of wise Alkinoös, as she was devising the return of great-hearted Odysseus. (8.7-9)

Thought: Athene takes on the guise of Alkinoös's herald. Her objective is not necessarily to trick the townspeople about anything but only to spread the news, which she could not possibly do in her true form without causing a stir.

(Odysseus, to Demodokos): 'Come to another part of the story, sing us the wooden horse, which Epeios made with Athene helping, the stratagem great Odysseus filled once with men and brought it to the upper city, and it was these men who sacked Ilion.' (8.492-495)

Thought: Odysseus uses his "disguise" to relive old memories and emotions. Notice, too, that he wants Demodokos to hurry up and get to the part of the story involving trickery!

(Polyphemos, in Odysseus's tale:) '"But tell me, so I may know: where did you put your well-made ship when you came? Nearby or far off?" 'So he spoke, trying me out, but I knew too much and was not deceived, but answered him in turn, and my words were crafty: "Poseidon, Shaker of the Earth, has shattered my vessel. He drove it against the rocks on the outer coast of your country, cracked on a cliff, it is gone, the wind on the sea took it [...]."' (9.279-285)

Thought: Odysseus's cunning is used primarily for purposes of survival.

(Odysseus, in his tale:) '"Nobody is my name. My father and mother call me Nobody, as do all the others who are my companions."' (9.366-367)

Thought: Odysseus's trick is the original "Who's on First?"

(Odysseus:) '[...] but I was planning so that things would come out the best way, and trying to find some release from death, for my companions and myself too, combining all my resource and treacheries, as with life at stake, for the great evil was very close to us. Ans as I thought, this was the plan that seemed best to me. There were some male sheep, rams, well nourished, thick and fleecy, handsome and large, with a large depth of wool. Silently I caught these and lashed them together with pliant willow withes, where the monstrous Cyclops lawless of mind had used to sleep. I had them in threes, and the one in the middle carried a man while the other two went on each side, so guarding my friends. Three rams carried each man, but as for myself, there was one ram, far the finest of all the flock.' (9.420-432)

Thought: Notice that, in times of worst trouble, Odysseus saves his own hide with his own cunning; he doesn't rely on Athene to magically appear and disguise him.

(Odysseus:) 'So she spoke to them, and the rest gave voice, and called her and at once she opened the shining doors, and came out, and invited them in, and all in their innocence entered; only Eurylochos waited outside, for he suspected treachery. She brought them inside and seated them on chairs and benches, and mixed them a potion, with barley and cheese and pale honey added to Pramneian wine, but put into the mixture malignant drugs, to make them forgetful of their own country. When she had given them this and they had drunk it down, next thing she struck them with her wand and drove them into her pig pens, and they took on the look of pigs, with the heads and voices and bristles of pigs, but the minds within them stayed as they had been before.' (10.229-241)

Thought: Deception in the *Odyssey* is always about appearances: Circe appears beautiful and benevolent, but is actually malicious. The men are made to appear as animals, but are actually still men in spirit and mind.

So speaking the goddess scattered the mist, and the land was visible. Long-suffering great Odysseus was gladdened then, rejoicing in the sight of his country, and kissed the grain-giving ground […]. (13.352-354)

Thought: Athene was actually hindering Odysseus's ability to see clearly – by disguising him in the cloud of mist, she blocks his ability to perceive accurately.

(Athene:) 'But come now, let me make you so that no mortal can recognize you. For I will wither the handsome flesh that is on your flexible limbs, and ruin the brown hair on your head, and about you put on such a clout of cloth any man will loathe when he sees you wearing it; I will dim those eyes, that have been so handsome, so you will be unprepossessing to all the suitors and your wife and child, those whom you left behind in your palace.' (13.396-403)

Thought: Odysseus's disguise as a beggar is much like Athene's former disguise as a mortal; by dressing below their stations, these two are able to test the integrity of those they deceive.

(Telemachos:) 'Suddenly you have changed, my friend, from what you were formerly; your skin is no longer as it was, you have other clothing. Surely you are one of those gods who hold the high heaven. Be gracious, then: so we shall give you favored offerings and golden gifts that have been well wrought. Only be merciful.' (16.181-185)

Thought: Interestingly, Telemachos finds it more believable that Odysseus is a god than that his father has finally returned home.

Around him the haughty suitors clustered. They all were speaking him fair, but in the depp of their hearts were devising evils. (17.65-66)

Thought: Deception is used for good but also for crime in the *Odyssey*.

(Odysseus:) 'So I will tell you the way of it, how it seems best to me. First, all go and wash, and put your tunics upon you, and tell the women in the palace to choose out their clothing. Then let the inspired singer take his clear-sounding lyre, and give us the lead for festive dance, so that anyone who is outside, some one of the neighbors, or a person going along the street, who hears us, will think we are having a wedding. Let no rumor go abroad in the town that the suitors have been murdered, until such time as we can make our way out to our estate with its many trees, and once there see what profitable plan the Olympian shows us.' (23.130-140)

Thought: Odysseus wants to trick all the Ithakans into thinking all the noise of the slaughter was the racket from a wedding celebration. How ironic, considering that was the very thing they wanted to avoid earlier.

Tradition and Custom Quotes

[Telemachos] saw Athene and went straight to the forecourt, the heart within him scandalized that a guest should still be standing at the doors. He stood beside her and took her by the right hand, and relieved her of the bronze spear, and spoke to her and addressed her in winged words: 'Welcome, stranger. You shall be entertained as a guest among us. Afterward, when you have tasted dinner, you shall tell us what your need is.' […] [A]nd he led her and seated her in a chair, with a cloth to sit on, the chair splendid and elaborate. For her feet there was a footstool. For himself, he drew a painted bench next her, apart from the others, the suitors, for fear the guest, made uneasy by the uproar, might lose his appetite there among overbearing people […]. (1.118-124, 130-134)

Thought: Telemachos shows his hospitality by inviting the guest in as soon as he sees him (well, technically "her," but Telemachos doesn't know that), refraining from asking his name and business, and immediately taking him inside, stowing away his effects, and feeding him at a fine table. He is thoughtful enough to consider the effect of the suitors' uncouth noise on his guest's appetite and locate him accordingly. In the following lines, we will see Telemachos's generosity illustrated by the amount of good food he serves to his guest. Of course, his actions are not totally altruistic. He wants news of his father from the guest, but we think this sounds like a pretty fair trade.

Then the haughty suitors came in, and all of them straightway took their places in order on chairs and along the benches, and their heralds poured water over their hands for them to wash with, and the serving maids brought them bread heaped up in the baskets, and the young men filled the mixing bowls with wine for their drinking. They put their hands to the good things that lay ready before them. But when they had put away their desire for eating and drinking, the suitors found their attention turned to other matters, the song and the dance; for these things

come at the end of the feasting. (1.144-152)

Thought: Immediately after Telemachos demonstrates the proper way to act, the suitors come in and demonstrate…the not-so-proper way. The fact that these two passages are placed right next to each other only highlights the contrast.

(Telemachos:) 'For all the greatest men who have the power in the islands, in Doulichion and Same and in wooded Zakynthos, and all who in rocky Ithaka are holders of lordships, all these are after my mother for marriage, and wear my house out. And she does not refuse the hateful marriage, nor is she able to make an end of the matter; and these eating up my substance waste it away; and soon they will break me myself to pieces.' (1.245-251)

Thought: Telemachos isn't just complaining about the obviously rude and disrespectful behavior of the suitors; he's complaining about a far more serious transgression: that they are breaking Zeus's rules of hospitality. He also hints at the impending plot against his life.

Telemachos replied: 'My guest, your words to me are very kind and considerate, what any father would say to his son. I shall not forget them. But come now, stay with me, eager though you are for your journey, so that you must first bathe and take your ease and, well rested and happy in your heart, then go back to your ship with a present, something prized, altogether fine, which will be your keepsake from me, what loving guests and hosts bestow on each other.' (1.307-313)

Thought: Telemachos shows his hospitality and gratefulness to Athene even though he does not know her true identity; this may be one of the reasons Athene disguises herself, to discern the true nature of various mortals. Clearly, Telemachos passed the test.

(Nestor:) 'May Zeus and all the other immortals beside forfend that you, in my domain, should go on back to your fast ship as from some man altogether poor and without clothing, who has not any abundance of blankets and rugs in his household for his guests, or for himself to sleep in soft comfort. But I do have abundance of fine rugs and blankets. No, no, in my house the dear son of Odysseus shall not have to go to sleep on the deck of a ship, as long as I am alive, and my sons after me are left in my palace to entertain our guests, whoever comes to my household.' (3.346-355)

Thought: Nestor shows great hospitality not only because of the Greek tradition, but because Telemachos is the son of his good friend.

(Nestor:) 'Act quickly now, dear children, and do me this favor, so that I may propitiate first of all the gods, Athene, who came plainly to me at our happy feasting in the god's honor. Come then, let one man go to the field for a cow, so that she may come with all speed, and let one of the oxherds be driving her, and one go down to the black ship of great-hearted Telemachos, and bring back all his companions, leaving only two beside her, and yet another go tell the worker in

gold Laerkes to come, so that he can cover the cow's horns with gold. You others stay here all together in a group but tell the serving women who are in the house to prepare a glorious dinner, and set chairs and firewood in readiness, and fetch bright water.' (3.418-429)

Thought: Feasting and sacrifice appear to be an intricate part of Greek hospitality, reminding us that the tradition has much to do with piety and reverence toward the gods.

(Menelaos:) 'Surely we two have eaten much hospitality from other men before we came back here. May Zeus only make an end of such misery hereafter. Unharness the strangers' horses then, and bring the men here to be feasted.' (4.33-36)

Thought: Menelaos's reasoning for his generous hospitality is one of gratitude for the assistance given him on his way home from Troy.

(Kalypso:) 'How is it, Hermes of the golden staff, you have come to me? I honor you and love you; but you have not come much before this. Speak what is in your mind. My heart is urgent to do it if I can, and if it is a thing that can be accomplished. But come in with me, so I can put entertainment before you.' So the goddess spoke, and she set before him a table which she had filled with ambrosia, and mixed red nectar for him. (5.87-93)

Thought: Even the gods have traditions of hospitality between one another.

(Nausikaa:) 'But now, since it is our land and our city that you have come to, you shall not lack for clothing nor anything else, of those gifts which should befall the unhappy suppliant on his arrival.' (6.191-193)

Thought: The generosity with which Odysseus is received by the Phaiakians recalls Telemachos's experience with the various kings he visits.

But when Alkinoös of the hallowed strength had heard this, he took by the hand the wise and much-devising Odysseus, and raised him up from the fireside, and set him in a shining chair, displacing for this powerful Laodamas, his son, who had been sitting next him and who was the one he loved most. A maidservant brought water for him and poured it from a splendid and golden pitcher, holding it above a silver basin for him to wash, and she pulled a polished table before him. A grave housekeeper brought in the bread and served it to him, adding many good things to it, generous with her provisions. Then long-suffering great Odysseus ate and drank. (7.167-177)

Thought: It is important to note that Odysseus receives this royal treatment before revealing his identity as the famous hero who helped the Greeks win the Trojan war. Much like Athene in disguise, he is treated well even in anonymity.

(Alkinoös:) 'Now, having feasted, go home and take your rest, and tomorrow at dawn we shall call the elders in, in greater numbers, and entertain the guest in our halls, and to the immortals accomplish fine sacrifices, and after that we shall think of conveyance, and how our guest without annoyance or hardship may come again, convoyed by us, to his own country, in happiness and speed, even though it lies very far off […].' (7.188-194)

Thought: Because he doesn't know who Odysseus is, Alkinoös's excessive hospitality is based purely on Greek tradition.

(Alkinoös:) 'Here is this stranger, I do not know who he is, come wandering suppliant here to my house from the eastern or western people. He urges conveyance, and entreats us for its assurance. So let us, as we have done before, hasten to convey him, for neither has any other man who has come to my house stayed here grieving a long time for the matter of convoy.' (8.28-33)

Thought: When Alkinoös refers to past visitors "to my house," we see that this is no special case of remarkable hospitality. Clearly, this is the norm for the generous Phaiakians.

(Laodamas:) 'Come you also now, father stranger, and try these contests, if you have skill in any. It beseems you to know athletics, for there is no greater glory that can befall a man living than what he achieves by speed of his feet or strength of his hands. So come then and try it, and scatter those cares that are on your spirit. Your voyage will not be put off for long, but now already your ship is hauled down to the sea, and your companions are ready.' (8.145-151)

Thought: We see from Laodamas that there are many different ways to show hospitality; it extends beyond mere provisions to friendly camaraderie.

(Odysseus:) 'Let any of the rest, whose heart and spirit are urgent for it, come up and try me, since you have irritated me so, either at boxing or wrestling or in a foot race, I begrudge nothing; any of the Phaiakians, that is, except Laodamas himself, for he is my host; who would fight with his friend? Surely any man can be called insensate and good for nothing who in an alien community offers to challenge his friend and host in the games. He damages what it is.' (8.204-211)

Thought: Odysseus shows the behavior of a good guest by refusing to challenge his host and protector. He places so much store by this that he compares it to the cutting away the ground from beneath one's feet; in other words, insulting one's host is akin to harming oneself.

(Alkinoös:) '[…] one who is your companion, and has thoughts honorable toward you, is of no less degree than a brother […].' (8.585-586)

Thought: The notion of hospitality is so strong in the world of the *Odyssey* that guests can even be considered part of one's family.

(Odysseus:) *'I had with me a goatskin bottle of black wine, sweet wine, given me by Maron, son of Euanthes and priest of Apollo, who bestrides Ismaros; he gave it because, respecting him with his wife and child, we saved them from harm. He made his dwelling among the trees of the sacred grove of Phoibos Apollo, and he gave me glorious presents. He gave me seven talents of well-wrought gold, and he gave me a mixing-bowl made all of silver, and gave along with it wine, drawing it off in storing jars, twelve in all. This was a sweet wine, unmixed, a divine drink.'* (9.196-205)

Thought: Odysseus reminds us that there is an exchange between host and guest: the guest must show kindness and good behavior, and the host returns the courtesy. This is why the suitors are not entitled to the hospitality of Telemachos and his mother.

'From the start my companions spoke to me and begged me to take some of the cheeses, come back again, and the next time to drive the lambs and kids from their pens, and get back quickly to the ship again, and go sailing off across the salt water; but I would not listen to them, it would have been better their way, not until I could see him, see if he would give me presents. My friends were to find the sight of him in no way lovely.' (9.224-230)

Thought: Odysseus faults his own logic here; he was operating on the assumption that whoever inhabited the cave would follow the traditional rules of hospitality. Of course, that wasn't the case here.

(Polyphemos, in Odysseus's tale:) *'"Stranger, you are a simple fool, or come from far off, when you tell me to avoid the wrath of the gods or fear them. The Cyclopes do not concern themselves over Zeus of the aegis, nor any of the rest of the blessed gods, since we are far better than they [...]."'* (9.273-287)

Thought: The punishment that Polyphemos ultimately suffers is justified by his refusal here to play by the rules. On the other hand, you could argue if Polyphemos and his people have chosen to live outside of Zeus's rules, why should they be forced to comply with them? This would be like traveling to another country and chastising them for not celebrating the Fourth of July. Again, the counter-argument would be that Zeus, as the King of the Gods, rules everything and everyone without question. What do you think?

(Polyphemos, in Odysseus's tale:) *'"Give me still more, frely, and tell me your name straightway now, so I can give you a guest present to make you happy."'* (9.355-356)

Thought: The Cyclops shows false hospitality towards Odysseus, promising him a lovely gift if he will tell him his name. Readers know that Polyphemos is untrustworthy and suspect a trick.

(Aiolos, in Odysseus's tale:) *"'O least of living creatures, out of this island! Hurry! I have no right to see on his way, none to give passage to any man whom the blessed gods hate with such bitterness. Out. This arrival means you are hateful to the immortals.'"* (10.72-75)

Thought: Aiolos no longer shows hospitality to Odysseus because he has squandered his gift.

(Odysseus:) *'So she spoke to them, and the rest gave voice, and called her and at once she opened the shining doors, and came out, and invited them in, and all in their innocence entered; only Eurylochos waited outside, for he suspected treachery. She brought them inside and seated them on chairs and benches, and mixed them a potion, with barley and cheese and pale honey added to Pramneian wine, but put into the mixture malignant drugs, to make them forgetful of their own country. When she had given them this and they had drunk it down, next thing she struck them with her wand and drove them into her pig pens, and they took on the look of pigs, with the heads and voices and bristles of pigs, but the minds within them stayed as they had been before.'* (10.229-241)

Thought: Circe's hospitality seems proper at first – before she changes her guests into pigs. Looks like the men should have looked this gift-horse in the mouth.

(Odysseus:) *'O great Alkinoös, pre-eminent among all people, there is a time for many words, and a time for sleeping; but if you insists of hearing me still, I would not begrudge you the tale of these happenings and others yet more pitiful to hear, the sorrows of my companions, who perished later, who escaped the onslaught and cry of battle, but perished all for the sake of a vile woman, on the homeward journey.'* (11.378-384)

Thought: Though it causes him pain, Odysseus tells his story in order to play the role of a good guest. He repays the generous hospitality with his words.

(Eumaios:) *'You too, old man of many sorrows, since the spirit brought you here to me, do not try to please me nor spell me with lying words. It is not for that I will entertain and befriend you, but for fear of Zeus, the god of guests, and for my own pity.'* (14.386-389)

Thought: Odysseus, for the first time, has proven an unworthy guest by telling lies to his host. Eumaios sees this, but overrides his hesitation at this dishonesty out of respect to Zeus. The rules of the gods, we see, are all-important.

The swineherd stood up to divide the portions, for he was fair minded, and separated all the meat into seven portions. One he set aside, with a prayer, for the nymphs and Hermes, the son of Maia, and the rest he distributed to each man, but gave Odysseus in honor the long cuts of the chine's portion of the white-toothed pig, and so exalted the heart of his master. (14.432-438)

Thought: Eumaios honors his guest like a king, taking the cuts usually saved for a lord from the meat and giving them to Odysseus. He also honors him in the same ritual with which he honors the gods, practically equating his guest to a divine being.

(Menelaos:) 'I would disapprove of another hospital man who was excessive in friendship, as of one excessive in hate. In all things balance is better.' (15.69-71)

Thought: Menelaos knows that a host can be just as ill-mannered by being too friendly when such behavior is not wanted by the guest. This is more complicated than we thought.

(Helen:) 'I too give you this gift, dear child: something to remember from Helen's hands, for your wife to wear at the lovely occasion of your marriage. Until that time let it lie away in your palace, in your dear mother's keeping […]. (15.125-128)

Thought: Helen shows her graciousness as a hostess by considering Telemachos's future and family when giving her gifts.

(Telemachos:) 'I will not willingly thrust you away from my balanced ship. Come, then, with me. There you will be entertained, from what we have left.' (15.280-281)

Thought: Telemachos shows hospitality even to a complete stranger. This means the laws of the gods are more important than the laws of the mortals.

(Penelope:) 'But come, handmaidens, give him a wash and spread a couch for him here, with bedding and coverlets and with shining blankets, so that he can keep warm as he waits for dawn of the golden throne, and early tomorrow you shall give him a bath, anoint him, so that he can sit in the hall beside Telemachos and expect to dine there; and it will be the worse for any of those men who inflicts heart-wasting annoyance on him; he will accomplish nothing here for all his terrible spite […].' (19.317-325)

Thought: Penelope is so generous that she offers a nameless beggar a place by Telemachos's side, simply for bringing her news of her husband.

Suffering Quotes

(Menelaos:) '[....] no one of the Achaians labored as much as Odysseus labored and achieved, and for him the end was grief for him, and for me a sorrow that is never forgotten for his sake, how he is gone so long, and we knew nothing of whether he is alive or dead.' (4.106-110)

Thought: There are many kinds of suffering in the *Odyssey*; compare Odysseus's trials on the sea to Menelaos's distress over his long-absent friend.

(Penelope:) 'Hear me, dear friends. The Olympian has given me sorrows beyond all others who were born and brought up together with me for first I lost a husband with the heart of a lion and who among the Danaans surpassed in all virtues, and great, whose fame goes wide through Hellas and midmost Argos; and now again the stormwinds have caught away my beloved son, without trace, from the halls, and I never heard when he left me. Hard-hearted, not one out of all of you then remembered to wake me out of my bed, though your minds knew all clearly, when he went out and away to board the hollow black ship. For if I had heard that he was considering this journey, then he would have had to stay, though hastening to his voyage, or he would have had to leave me dead in the halls.' (4.722-735)

Thought: Penelope, like Menelaos, acknowledges suffering. However, unlike the Spartan King, she is more concerned over Odysseus's anguish than her own.

By nights he would lie beside her, of necessity, in the hollow caerns, against his will, by one who was willing, but all the days he would sit upon the rocks, at the seaside, breaking his heart in tears and lamentation and sorrow as weeping tears he looked out over the barren water. (5.154-158)

Thought: Odysseus has everything he could possibly want with Kalypso: eternal youth, luxury, prosperity, and sex – but still, he yearns for the trials of mortal life.

(Kalypso:) '[…] but if you only knew in your own heart how many hardships you were fated to undergo before getting back to your country, you would stay here with me and be the lord of this household and be an immortal […].' (5.206-209)

Thought: Kalypso has a point – Odysseus intentionally *chooses* suffering. In this, he parallels Achilleus, the hero of *The Iliad*, who faces a choice between a long life back home and a short, glorious life fighting at Troy—and chooses Option II. And yet, Odysseus's suffering is for the sake of getting back home—exactly what Achilleus rejects.

(Odysseus:) '[…] what I want and all my days I pine for is to go back to my house and see my day of homecoming. And if some god batters me far out on the wine-blue water, I will endure it, keeping a stubborn spirit inside me, for already I have suffered much and done much hard work on the waves and in the fighting. So let this adventure follow.' (5.219-224)

Thought: Odysseus seems to think he's seen it all. There's nothing he can't handle, he says, in order to get home to Ithaka.

(Odysseus:) 'Ah me unhappy, what in the long outcome will befall me? I fear the goddess might have spoken the truth in all ways when she said that on the sea and before I came to my country I would go through hardships; now all this is being accomplished, such clouds are these, with which Zeus is cramming the wide sky and has staggered the sea, and stormblasts of winds from every direction are crowding in. My sheer destruction is certain.' (5.299-305)

Thought: Odysseus despairs at the first storm sent his way by Poseidon after he leaves Kalypso's island. So much for taking suffering in stride.

(Odysseus:) 'What will happen now, and what in the long outcome will befall me? For if I wait out the uncomfortable night by the river, I fear that the female dew and the evil frost together will be too much for my damaged strength, I am so exhausted and in the morning a chilly wind will blow from the river; but if I go up the slope and into the shadowy forest, and lie down to sleep among the dense bushes, even if the chill and weariness let me be, and a sweet sleep comes upon me, I fear I may become spoil and prey to the wild animals.' (5.465-473)

Thought: Odysseus wavers between his fear of suffering and his determination to endure.

(Nausikaa:) '[…] it is Zeus himself, the Olympian, who gives people good fortune, to each single man, to the good and the bad, just as he wishes; and since he must have given you yours, you must even endure it.' (6.188-190)

Thought: Nausikaa shows maturity beyond her age by wisely telling Odysseus he must bear all the suffering sent his way.

So the famous singer sang his tale, but Odysseus melted, and from under his eyes the tears ran down, drenching his cheeks. As a woman weeps, lying over the body of her dear husband, who fell fighting for her city and people as he tried to beat off the pitiless day from city and children; she sees him dying and gasping for breath, and winding her body about him she cries high and shrill, while the men behind her, hitting her with their spear butts on the back and the shoulders, force her up and lead her away into slavery, to have hard work and sorrow, and her cheeks are wracked with pitiful weeping. Such were the pitiful tears Odysseus shed from under his brows, but they went unnoticed by all the others […]. (8.521-532)

Thought: Odysseus relives his suffering from Troy vicariously through the narrative of Demodokos. Even the mere memory of hardship is painful to endure.

Thought: Circe is referring here to the monster Skylla, but you can really apply her words to all forms of suffering. Pain, she tells Odysseus, is unavoidable.

(Eurylochos, in Odysseus's tale:) "'Listen to what I say, my companions, though you are suffering evils. All deaths are detestable for wretched mortals, but hunger is the sorriest way to die and encounter fate. Come then, let us cut out the best of Helios' cattle, and sacrifice them to the immortals who hold wide heaven, and if we ever come back to Ithaka, land of our fathers, presently we will build a rich temple to the Sun God Helios Hyperion, and store it with dedications, many and good. But if, in anger over his high-horned cattle, he wishes to wreck our ship, and the rest of the gods stand by him, I would far rather gulp the waves and lose my life in them once for all, than be pinched to death on this desolate island.'" (12.340-351)

Thought: Eurylochos considers starvation the worst death of all and prefers to commit a crime against heaven than suffer so.

(Athene:) '[I will] tell you all the troubles you are destined to suffer in your well-wrought house; but you must, of necessity, endure all, and tell no one out of all the men and the women that you have come back from your wanderings, but you must endure much grief in silence, standing and facing men in their violence.' (13.306-310)

Thought: Again, the message is to endure suffering as it can not be avoided. Of course, Odysseus will just be biding his time until he can deliver some *serious* (and seemingly excessive) payback.

(Odysseus:) 'There is nothing worse for mortal men than the vagrant life, but still for the sake of the cursed stomach people endure hard sorrows, when roving and pain and grief befall them.' (15.343-345)

Thought: Odysseus seems to agree with his men that hunger is the worst kind of suffering.

(Eumaios:) 'All too much with enduring heart she does wait for him there in your own palace, and always with her the wretched nights and the days also waste her away with weeping.' (16.37-39)

Thought: Penelope's grieving is implicitly compared to that of Odysseus.

(Eumaios:) 'Shall I on the same errand go with the news to wretched Laertes, who while he so greatly grieved for Odysseus yet would look after his farm and with the thralls in his household would eat and drink, whenever the spirit was urgent with him; but now, since you went away in the ship to Pylos, they say he has not eaten in this way, nor drunk anything, nor looked to his farm, but always in lamentation and mourning sits grieving, and the flesh on his bones is wasting from him.' (16.137-145)

Thought: Laertes mental anguish has rendered him immobile and ineffective.

(Penelope:) 'How I wish chaste Artemis would give me a death so soft, and now, so I would not go on in my heart grieving all my life, and longing for love of a husband excellent in every virtue, since he stood out among the Achaians.' (18.202-205)

Thought: This is an uncharacteristic moment of weakness for the usually patient Penelope.

(Penelope:) 'So I wish that they who have their homes on Olympos would make me vanish, or sweet-haired Artemis strike me, so that I could meet the Odysseus I long for, even under the hateful earth, and not have to please the mind of an inferior husband. Yet the evil is endurable, when one cries through the days, with heart constantly troubled, yet still is taken by sleep in the nights; for sleep is oblivion of all things, both good and evil, when it has shrouded the eyelids. But now the god has sent the evil dreams thronging upon me. For on this very night there was one who lay by me, like him as he was when he went with the army, so that my own heart was happy. I thought it was no dream, but a waking vision.' (20.79-90)

Thought: Penelope suffers so painfully for the loss of Odysseus that even her dreams are haunted by his absence.

He spoke, and the black cloud of sorrow closed on Laertes. In both hands he caught up the grimy dust and poured it over his face and grizzled head, groaning incessantly. The spirit rose up in Odysseus, and now in his nostrils there was a shock of bitter force as he looked on his father. He sprang to him and embraced and kissed and then said to him: 'Father, I am he, the man you ask about.' (24.315-321)

Thought: The *Odyssey* reminds us that to witness the suffering of others is painful in itself.

Principles Quotes

(Telemachos:) 'I should not have sorrowed so over his dying if he had gone down among his companions in the land of the Trojans, or in the arms of his friends, after he had wound up the fighting. So all the Achaians would have heaped a grave mound over him, and he would have won great fame for himself and his son hereafter. But now ingloriously the stormwinds have caught and carried him away, out of sight, out of knowledge, and he left pain and lamentation to me.' (1.236-243)

Thought: Telemachos holds the common belief that a death in arms is noble and honorable.

(Telemachos:) 'For my mother, against her will, is beset by suitors, own sons to the men who are greatest hereabouts. These shrink from making the journey to the house of her father Ikarios, so that he might take bride gifts for his daughter and bestow her on the one he wished,

who came as his favorite; rather, all their days, they come and loiter in our house and sacrifice our oxen and our sheep and our fat goats and make a holiday feast of it and drink the bright wine recklessly. Most of our substance is wasted.' (2.50-58)

Thought: Telemachos basically accuses the suitors of dishonor. His anger at them is justified by the fact that they have violated basic Greek principles.

(Telemachos:) 'Antinoös, I cannot thrust the mother who bore me, who raised me, out of the house against her will. My father, alive or dead, is elsewhere in the world. It will be hard to pay back Ikarios, if willingly I dismiss my mother. I will suffer some evil from her father, and the spirit will give me more yet, for my mother will call down her furies upon me as she goes out of the house, and I shall have the people's resentment.' (2.130-137)

Thought: Telemachos uses notions of honor and principle in his reasoning.

(Mentor:) 'Now it is not so much the proud suitors I resent for doing their violent acts by their minds' evil devising; for they lay their hands on the line when violently they eat up the house of Odysseus, who, they say to themselves, will not come back; but now I hold it against you other people, how you all sit there in silence, and never with an assault of words try to check the suitors, though they are so few, and you so many.' (2.235-241)

Thought: Mentor points out the cowardice (and hence dishonor) of the majority, who stay silent out of fear and respect for the suitors. They passively dishonor Odysseus by not standing up for the proper treatment of his family and household.

(Peisistratos:) 'My guest, make your prayer now to the lord Poseidon, for his is the festival you have come to on your arrival; but when you have poured to him and prayed, according to custom, then give this man also a cup of the sweet wine, so that he too can pour, for I think he also will make his prayer to the immortals. All men need the gods. But this one is a younger man than you, and of the same age as I am. This is why I am first giving you the goblet.' (3.43-50)

Thought: Peisistratos honors both seniority and the gods with his gesture; because this is done before Athene, he is soon rewarded for his action.

(Menelaos:) '[…] and sitting well in order we dashed the oars in the gray sea, back to where Egypt is, the sky-fallen river, and there I stranded my ships, and there I rendered complete hecatombs. But when I had ended the anger of the gods, who are everlasting, I piled a mound for Agamemnon, so that his memory might never die. I did this, and set sail, and the immortals gave me a wind, so brought me back to my own dear country with all speed.' (4.580-587)

Thought: Proper burial rites are a big deal in this culture, as we see over and over in the *Odyssey*. A man is only honored in death when he is properly respected by those still living.

(Athene, disguised as Iphthime:) '*As for that other one, I will not tell you the whole story whether he lives or has died. It is bad to babble emptily.*' *(4.836-837)*

Thought: Athene displays her own sense of honor by refusing to speak falsely to Penelope.

(Kalypso:) '*Earth be my witness in this, and the wide heaven above us, and the dripping water of the Styx, which oath is the biggest and most formidable oat among the blessed immortals, that this is no other painful trial I am planning against you […]*' *(5.184-187)*

Thought: The fact that Odysseus is willing to trust Kalypso solely on the basis of her words reminds us of how important notions of honor are in the *Odyssey*.

(Odysseus:) '*Three times and four times happy those Danaans were who died then in wide Troy land, bringing favor to the sons of Atreus, as I wish I too had died at that time and met my destiny on the day when the greatest number of Trojans threw their bronze-headed weapons upon me, over the body of perished Achilleus, and I would have had my rites and the Achaians given me glory. Now it is by a dismal death that I must be taken.*' *(5.306-312)*

Thought: Odysseus wishes he could've had more honor by dying in the battlefields of Troy, fighting alongside his men for his king. Instead, he thinks he is fated to die ingloriously at sea, be denied a decent burial, and have his reputable name forgotten.

(Odysseus:) '*Stand as you are, girls, a little away from me, so that I can wash the salt off my shoulders and use the olive oil on them. It is long since my skin has known any ointment. But I will not bathe in front of you, for I feel embarrassed in the presence of lovely-haired girls to appear all naked.*' *(6.218-222)*

Thought: Odysseus respects social boundaries with respect to these young girls. He is too honorable (or rather, "em-bare-assed") to allow them to see him naked.

(Odysseus:) '*Then I shoved the beam underneath a deep bed of cinders, waiting for it to heat, and I spoke to all my companions in words of courage, so none should be in a panic, and back out […].*' *(9.375-377)*

Thought: In the *Odyssey*, honor is proven by showing courage in the face of adversity; Odysseus urges his men to action on the grounds that they must do just this.

(Odysseus:) 'But when the young dawn showed again with her rosy fingers, then I sent my companions away to the house of Circe to bring back the body of Elpenor, who had died there. Then we cut logs, and where the extreme of the foreland jutted out, we buried him, sorrowful, shedding warm tears for him. But when the dead man had burned and the dead man's armor, piling the grave mound and pulling the gravestone to stand above it, we planted the well-shaped oar in the very top of the grave mound.' (12.8-15)

Thought: Odysseus honors the dead Elpenor by setting up a proper burial for him. This ensures that he will not be forgotten among the living and will have respect among the dead.

(Odysseus:) 'I wish that I were truly as young as I am in spirit, or a son of stately Odysseus were here, or he himself might come in from his wandering. There is time still for hope. If such things could be, another could strike my head from my shoulders if I did not come as an evil thing to all those people as I entered the palace of Odysseus, the son of Laertes. And if I, fighting alone, were subdued by all their number, then I would rather die, cut down in my own palace, than to have to go on watching forever these shameful activities, guests being battered about, or to see them rudely mishandling the serving women all about the beautiful palace, to see them drawing the wine and eating up food in this utterly reckless way, without end, forever and always at it.' (16.99-111)

Thought: Odysseus advises Telemachos that it is more honorable to die fighting on one's feet than to live tolerating such behavior from the suitors. Honor, then, is valued above life in the *Odyssey*.

(Penelope:) 'But tell Autonoë and Hippodameia to come, so that they can stand at my side in the great hall. I will not go alone among men. I think that immodest.' (18.182-184)

Thought: Penelope shows a woman's sense of honor by refusing to show herself to a roomful of men alone and unattended by maids. Honor for a woman is different than honor for a man in the *Odyssey*.

(Penelope:) 'Human beings live for only a short time, and when a man is harsh himself, and his mind knows harsh thoughts, all men pray that sufferings will befall him hereafter while he lives; and when he is dead all men make fun of him. But when a man is blameless himself, and his thoughts are blameless, the friends he has entertained carry his fame widely to all mankind, and many are they who call him excellent.' (19.328-334)

Thought: Penelope rightly recognizes the value of honor and reputation – this is one of the reasons she is so adamant about keeping loyal to her husband.

(Telemachos:) 'But if you are determined to murder me with the sharp bronze, then that would be my wish also, since it would be far better than to have to go on watching forever these shameful activities, guests being battered about, or to see you rudely mishandling the serving all about the beautiful palace.' (20.315-319)

Thought: Telemachos shows that he has indeed learned Odysseus's lessons on honor; he would, like his father, rather die fighting than live humiliated.

Then the thoughtful Telemachos said to him in answer: 'Father, it was my own mistake, and there is no other to blame. I left the door of the chamber, which can close tightly, open at an angle. One of these men was a better observer than I.' (22.153-157)

Thought: Telemachos shows his honor by owning up to the fact that the mistake was his and that it had its consequences. He does not try to hide his guilt or blame others.

(Agamemnon:) 'So, even now you have died, you have not lost your name, but always in the sight of all mankind your fame shall be great, Achilleus.' (24.92-94)

Thought: Agamemnon reminds Achilleus that honor is forever, unlike the passing glory of life. Because of his actions, Achilleus has earned immortality for his name. Still, Achilleus's earlier comments suggest that he doesn't agree with this: he would rather be unremarkable and alive.

Laertes also rejoiced, and said to them: 'What day is this for me, dear gods? I am very happy. My son and my son's son are contending over their courage.' (24.513-515)

Thought: Laertes feels a surge of pride and honor to see himself the ancestor of two such strapping and courageous young men. They have brought honor back to his family's name.

Loyalty Quotes

So he spoke and the dear nurse Eurykleia cried out, and bitterly lamenting she addressed him in winged words: 'Why, my beloved child, has this intention come into your mind? Why do you wish to wander over much country, you, an only and loved son? Illustrious Odysseus has perished far from his country in some outlandish region. And these men will devise evils against you, on your returning, so you shall die by guile, and they divide all that is yours. No, but stay here and guard your possessions. It is not right for you to wander and suffer hardships on the barren wide sea.' (2.361-370)

Thought: Eurykleia's loyalty to Odysseus's household is seen in her love for Telemachos, whom she treats like her own son.

[…] the sweet lifetime was draining out of him, as he wept for a way home, since the nymph was no longer pleasing to him. By nights he would lie beside her, of necessity, in the hollow caverns, against his will, by one who was willing, but all the days he would sit upon the rocks, at the seaside, breaking his heart in tears and lamentation and sorrow as weeping tears he looked out over the barren water. (5.152-158)

Thought: Odysseus's desire for Kalypso has been trumped by his loyalty to Penelope.

(Nausikaa:) 'A while ago he seemed an unpromising man to me. Now he even resembles one of the gods, who hold high heaven. If only the man to be called my husband could be like this one, a man living here, if only this one were pleased to stay here.' (6.242-245)

Thought: Since we know Odysseus has no qualms about sleeping around on Penelope, we have to wonder why he holds no interest in the obviously beautiful Nausikaa. Might it have something to do with being a good guest? Hmm…

(Athene, disguised as the little girl:) 'So she was held high in the heart and still she is so, by her beloved children, by Alkinoös himself, and by the people, who look toward her as to a god when they see her, and speak in salutation as she walks about in her city. For there is no good intelligence that she herself lacks. She dissolves quarrels, even among men, when she favors them.' (7.69-74)

Thought: Loyalty here is merit-based; the Phaiakians don't revere their Queen because of her title, rather it is because of her "grace" and "wisdom."

(Odysseus:) '[…] the gods brought me to the island Ogygia, where Kalypso lives, with ordered hair, a dread goddess, and she received me and loved me excessively and cared for me, and she promised to make me an immortal and all my days to be ageless, but never so could she win over the heart within me.' (7.254-258)

Thought: Odysseus's claim that he "never gave consent" is worth a closer look. He seems to be saying that he passively gave into Kalypso, yet never truly desired to be with her.

There, shedding tears, he [Odysseus] went unnoticed by all the others, but Alkinoös alone understood what he did and noticed, since he was sitting next to him and heard him groaning heavily. (8.93-95)

Thought: Odysseus's persistent loyalty to his fallen comrades is shown in his grief over their memories.

[Hephaistos, in Demodokos' tale:] "'Father Zeus and all you other blessed immortal gods, come here, to see a ridiculous sight, no seemly matter, how Aphrodite daughter of Zeus forever holds me in little favor, but she loves ruinous Ares because he is handsome, and goes sound on his feet, while I am misshapen from birth, and for this I hold no other responsible but my own father and mother, and I wish they never had got me.'" (8.306-312)

Thought: Demodokos' story is an illustration of infidelity to one's spouse with an implicit message for men and women not to cheat on their true loves. This unfaithful Aphrodite contrasts sharply with the staunchly loyal Penelope.

So the famous singer sang his tale, but Odysseus melted, and from under his eyes the tears ran down, drenching his cheeks. As a woman weeps, lying over the body of her dear husband, who fell fighting for her city and people as he tried to beat off the pitiless day from city and children; she sees him dying and gasping for breath, and winding her her body about him she cries high and shrill, while the men behind her, hitting her with their spear butts on the back and the shoulders, force her up and lead her away into slavery, to have hard work and sorrow, and her cheeks are wracked with pitiful weeping. Such were the pitiful tears Odysseus shed from under his brows [...]. (8.521-532)

Thought: This epic simile shows the depth of love and emotion between a husband and wife. This is one of major the bonds of loyalty we see in the *Odyssey*, along with loyalty to one's children and to comrades.

(Odysseus:) 'My men went on and presently met the Lotus-Eaters, nor did these Lotus-Eaters have any thoughts of destroying our companions, but they only gave them lotus to taste of. But any of them who ate the honey-sweet fruit of lotus was unwilling to take any message back, or to go away, but they wanted to stay there with the lotus-eating people, feeding on lotus, and forget the way home.' (9.91-97)

Thought: On one level, the Lotus blossoms represent ALL the temptation the men face on their return to Ithaka. While this is the most direct threat to men's loyalty to their homes, episodes like Circe's treachery and the Sirens' song present similar dangers.

(Odysseus:) 'Nevertheless we sailed on, night and day, for nine days, and on the tenth at last appeared the land of our fathers, and we could see people tending fires, we were very close to them. But then the sweet sleep came upon me, for I was worn out with always handling the sheet myself, and I could not give it to any other companion, so we could come home quicker to our own country; but my companions talked with each other and said that I was bringing silver and gold home with me, given me by great-hearted Aiolos, son of Hippotas; [...] and the evil counsel of my companions prevailed, and they opened the bag and the winds all burst out.' (10.28-36, 46-47)

Thought: The Ithakans allow curiosity to trump their loyalty to their master Odysseus.

(Odysseus, in his tale:) "'Oh, Circe, how could any man in his right mind ever endure to taste of the food and drink that are set before him, until with his eyes he saw his companions set free? So then, if you are sincerely telling me to eat and drink, set them free, so my eyes can again behold my eager companions.'" (10.383-387)

Thought: Odysseus, loyal to his comrades, puts their safety before his own, risking his own neck to save their hides.

(Odysseus:) 'But first there came the soul of my companion, Elpenor, for he had not yet been buried under earth of the wide ways, since we had left his body behind in Circe's palace, unburied and unwept, with this other errand before us. I broke into tears at the sight of him, and my heart pitied him […].' (11.51-56)

Thought: In the *Odyssey*, loyalty is important both before and after death.

(Agamemnon, in Odysseus's tale:) '[…] most pitiful was the voice I heard of Priam's daughter Kassandra, killed by treacherous Klytaimestra over me; but I lifted my hands and with them beat on the ground as I died upon the sword, but the sluttish woman turned away from me and was so hard that her hands would not press shut my eyes and mouth though I was going to Hades'. So there is nothing more deadly or more vile than a woman who stores her mind with acts that are of such sort, as this one did when she thought of this act of dishonor, and plotted the murder of her lawful husband. See, I had been thinking that I would be welcome to my children and thralls of my household when I came home, but she with thoughts surpassingly grisly splashed the shame on herself and the rest of her sex, on women still to come, even on the one whose acts are virtuous.' (11.421-434)

Thought: Where Penelope is a steadfast symbol of loyalty, Klytaimestra is quite the opposite. She betrays her lord by taking a lover in his absence and shows her treachery by killing her husband when he returns. She so hates him that she refuses to honor the rights of the dead – closing his eyes or shutting his lips so that he may be granted passage to the Underworld. So embittered is Agamemnon by her betrayal that he condemns all women on the grounds that they have the same sort of treachery in them.

(The Sirens, in Odysseus's tale:) "'Come this way, honored Odysseus, great glory of the Achaians, and stay your ship, so that you can listen here to our singing; for no one else has ever sailed past this place in his black ship until he has listened to the honey-sweet voice that issues from our lips; then goes on, well-pleased, knowing more than ever he did; for we know everything that the Argives and Trojans did and suffered in wide Troy through the gods' despite. Over all the generous earth we know everything that happens." So they sang, in sweet utterance, and the heart within me desired to listen, and I signaled my companions to set me free, nodding with my brows, but they leaned on and rowed hard, and Perimedes and

Eurylochos, rising up, straightway fastened me with even more lashings and squeezed me together.' (12.184-196)

Thought: The Sirens represent temptation in its basest form – longing for beauty and lust for women. Temptations like these threaten the loyalty of Odysseus and the other Ithakans.

(Odysseus:) 'Right in her doorway she [Skylla] ate them up. They were screaming and reaching out their hands to me in this horrid encounter. That was the most pitiful scene that these eyes have looked on in my sufferings as I explored the routes over the water.' (12.256-259)

Thought: Because of the loyalty and compassion he holds for his men, Odysseus cites bearing witness to their death the worst suffering he encounters.

(Eumaios:) '[…] any vagrant who makes his way to the land of Ithaka goes to my mistress and babbles his lies to her, and she then receives him well and entertains him and asks him everything, and as she mourns him the tears run down from her eyes, since this is the right way for a wife when her husband has perished.' (14.126-130)

Thought: Penelope's actions are driven by her loyalty for her husband – perhaps this loyalty is the very reason she refuses to accept the common (and, given the length of his absence, quite *reasonable*) belief that he is dead.

(Eumaios:) '[…] but the longing is on me for Odysseus, and he is gone from me; and even when he is not here, my friend, I feel some modesty about naming him, for in his heart he cared for me greatly and loved me. So I call him my master, though he is absent.' (14.144-147)

Thought: Eumaios is so loyal to Odysseus that, despite the common notion that the man is dead, he still considers him lord and master.

Only the swineherd did not please to leave his pigs, and go to bed indoors, but made preparations as he went out; and Odysseus was happy that his livelihood was so well cared for while he was absent. (14.524-527)

Thought: Odysseus is impressed by Eumaios's devotion to his craft – even though it is something as simple as caring for swine – because it shows a loyalty to the well-being of Odysseus's household even during his absence.

(Eumaios:) 'From the heart she [Penelope] loved me dearly. Now I go lacking all these things, but the blessed immortals prosper all the work that I myself do abiding here, whence I eat and drink and give to people I honor; but there is no sweet occasion now to hear from my mistress in word or fact, since the evil has fallen upon our household […].' (15.370-375)

Thought: Many of the servants in Odysseus's house hold a familial loyalty for the royal family.

He came up to meet his master, and kissed his head, and kissed too his beautiful shining eyes, and both his hands, and the swelling tear fell from him. And as a father, with heart full of love, welcomes his only and grown son, for whose sake he has undergone many hardships when he comes back in the tenth year from a distant country, so now the noble swineherd, clinging fast to godlike Telemachos, kissed him even as if he had escaped dying [...].' (16.14-21)

Thought: This epic simile makes it obvious that Eumaios loves Telemachos like a son; at this moment, then, he acts as a substitute for Odysseus, who cannot yet show this sort of emotion for his son.

There the dog Argos lay in the dung, all covered with dog ticks. Now, as he perceived that Odysseus had come close to him, he wagged his tail, and laid both his ears back; only he now no longer had the strength to move any closer to his master, who, watching him from a distance, without Eumaios noticing, secretly wiped a tear away [...]. (17.300-305)

Thought: Argos demonstrates the unconditional love and loyalty of servant for master; Homer seems to present this, the emotion of a simple creature, as the most ideal, least adulterated form of loyalty.

(Phemios:) 'I am at your knees, Odysseus. Respect me, have mercy. You will be sorry in time to come if you kill the singer of songs. I sing to the gods and to human people, and I am taught by myself, but the god has inspired in me the song-ways of every kind. I am such a one as can sing before you as to a god. Then do not be furious to behead me. Telemachos, too, your own dear son, would tell you, as I do, that it was against my will, and with no desire on my part, that I served the suitors here in your house and sang at their feasting. They were too many and too strong, and they forced me to do it.' So he spoke, and the hallowed prince Telemachos heard him. Quickly then he spoke to his father, who stood close by him: 'Hold fast. Do not strike this man with the bronze. He is innocent. And let us spare Medon our herald, a man who has always taken care of me when I was a child in your palace [...].' (22.344-358)

Thought: Telemachos shows compassion and mercy for the innocent who deserve it. He returns the loyalty of his servants in kind.

She spoke, and still more roused in him the passion for weeping. He wept as he held his lovely wife, whose thoughts were virtuous. And as when the land appears welcome to men who are swimming, after Poseidon has smashed their strong-built ship on the open water, pounding it with the weight of wind and the heavy seas, and only a few escape the gray water landward by swimming, with a thick scurf of salt coated upon them, and gladly they set foot on the shore, escaping the evil; so welcome was her husband to her as she looked upon him, and she could not let him go from the embrace of her white arms. (23.231-240)

Thought: Appropriately, Homer describes this emotion like the love of a nearly-drowned swimmer (a role Odysseus has filled many times) for the solid earth (which Penelope represents simply through her constancy as a faithful woman).

Perseverance Quotes

(Telemachos:) 'If only the gods would give me such strength as he has to take revenge on the suitors for their overbearing oppression. They force their way upon me and recklessly plot against me. No, the gods have spun out no such strand of prosperity for me and my father. Now we must even have to endure it.' (3.205-209)

Thought: Despite Telemachos's burning desire to avenge himself on the suitors at his house, he perseveres in his patience, trusting justice to the gods' will. He also makes explicit Homer's comparison of Agamemnon's story to that of Odysseus.

(Odysseus, in his tale:) '"Dear friends, surely we are not unlearned in evils. This is no greater evil now than it was when the Cyclops had us cooped in his hollow cave by force and violence, but even there, by my courage and counsel and my intelligence, we escaped away. I think that all this will be remembered some day too. Then do as I say, let us all be won over."' (12.208-213)

Thought: Odysseus urges his men to have courage because they have persevered through worse dangers than this (Skylla and Charybdis). His determination incites that of his men.

(Eurylochos, in Odysseus's tale:) '"You are a hard man, Odysseus. Your force is greater, your limbs never wear out. You must be made all of iron, when you will not let your companions, worn with hard work and wanting sleep, set foot on this land, where if we did, on the seagirt island we could once more make ready a greedy dinner; but you force us to blunder along just as we are through the running night, driven from the island over the misty face of the water."' (12.279-285)

Thought: Eurylochos considers Odysseus superhuman for his ability to endure more hardship than, well, any other mortal man could. His perseverance is exceptional; after enduring the horrors of Skylla and Charybdis, he still has the fortitude to tell his crew to sail on past a potentially safe island retreat for the night.

(Odysseus:) 'At this time Charybdis sucked down the sea's salt water, but I reached high in the air above me, to where the tall fig tree grew, and caught hold of it and clung like a bat; there was no place where I could firmly brace my feet, or climb up it, for the roots of it were far from me, and the branches hung out far, big and long branches that overshadowered Charybdis. Inexorably I hung on, waiting for her to vomit the keel and mast back up again. I longed for them, and they came late; at the time when a man leaves the law court, for dinner, after judging the many disputes brought him by litigious young men; that was the time it took the timbers to

appear from Charybdis.' (12.431-441)

Thought: Odysseus shows not only his mental but also his physical perseverance. That said, his physical prowess would be nothing without his incredible willpower.

(Odysseus:) 'Of all creatures that breathe and walk on the earth there is nothing more helpless than a man is, of all that the earth fosters; for he thinks that he will never suffer misfortune in future days, while the gods grant him courage, and his knees have spring in them. But when the blessed gods bring sad days upon him, against his will he must suffer it with enduring spirit. For the mind in men upon earth goes according to the fortunes the Father of Gods and Men, day by day, bestows upon them.' (18.130-137)

Thought: Odysseus comments that when the gods throw bad luck at a man, there is nothing for him to do other than simply endure and hope for the best. He must persevere to survive the pain.

'[…] and out of the palace issued those women who in the past had been going to bed with the suitors, full of cheerful spirits and greeting each other with laughter. But the spirit deep in the heart of Odysseus was stirred by this, and much he pondered in the division of mind and spirit, whether to spring on them and kill each one, or rather to let them lie this one more time with the insolent suitors, for the last and latest time; but the heart was growling within him.' (20.6-13)

Thought: Odysseus is enraged at the betrayal of trust these harlots commit. It's bad enough that the suitors traitorously enjoy food at Odysseus's expense, but these women now pleasure them, turning their backs on Odysseus's kindness and reputation.

Thought: Odysseus comments joyfully that both he and his wife have persevered through all obstacles – and that, by stealing, he can replenish his stock of sheep! How romantic.

Family Quotes

(Telemachos:) 'For my mother, against her will, is beset by suitors, own sons to the men who are greatest hereabouts. These shrink from making the journey to the house of her father Ikarios, so that he might take bride gifts for his daughter and bestow her on the one he wished, who came as his favorite; rather, all their days, they come and loiter in our house and sacrifice our oxen and our sheep and our fat goats and make a holiday feast of it and drink the bright wine recklessly. Most of our substance is wasted.' (2.50-58)

Thought: One sign of the suitors shamefulness—aside from the fact that they are eating up all of Odysseus's stuff—is that they don't even have the guts to go and ask Penelope's dad for her hand in marriage. This just proves even further that they have no respect for family obligations.

They came into the cavernous hollow of Lakedaimon and made their way to the house of glorious Menelaos. They found him in his own house giving, for many townsmen, a wedding feast for his son and his stately daughter. The girl he was sending to the son of Achilleus, breaker of battalions, for in Troy land first he had nodded his head to it and promised to give her, and now the gods were bringing to pass their marriage; so he was sending her on her way, with horses and chariots, to the famous city of the Myrmidons, where Neoptolemos was lord, and he brought Alektor's daughter from Sparta, to give powerful Megapenthes, his young grown son born to him by a slave woman; but the gods gave no more children to Helen once she had borned her first and only child, the lovely Hermione, with the beauty of Aphrodite the golden. (4.1-14)

Thought: Menelaos obviously honors his family because he throws wedding feasts for both his son and daughter. That, and he's really loaded.

(Helen:) 'Shall I be wrong, or am I speaking the truth? My heart tells me to speak, for I think I never saw such a likeness, neither in man nor woman, and wonder takes me as I look on him, as this man has a likeness to the son of great-hearted Odysseus, Telemachos, who was left behind in the house, a young child by that man when, for the sake of shameless me, the Achaians went beneath Troy, their hearts intent upon reckless warfare.' (4.140-146)

Thought: Telemachos has the handsome appearance of his renowned father, but more importantly has inherited Odysseus's character.

(Menelaos:) 'Dear friend, since you have said all that a man who is thoughtful could say or do, even one who was older than you are— why, this is the way your father is, so you too speak thoughtfully. Easily recognized is the line of that man, for whom Kronos' son weaves good fortune in his marrying and begetting, as now he has given to Nestor, all his days, for himself to grow old prosperously in his own palace, and also that his sons should be clever and excellent in the spear's work.' (4.204-212)

Thought: The family resemblance is as strong between Peisistratos and Nestor as it is between Telemachos and Odysseus—but this time Menelaos recognizes the son through his words, not merely his appearance.

(Menelaos:) '[…] and sitting well in order we dashed the oars in the gray sea, back to where Egypt is, the sky-fallen river, and there I stranded my ships, and there I rendered complete hecatombs. But when I had ended the anger of the gods, who are everlasting, I piled a mound for Agamemnon, so that his memory might never die. I did this, and set sail, and the immortals gave me a wind, so brought me back to my own dear country with all speed.' (4.580-587)

Thought: Menelaos shows respect for his kin by honoring his murdered brother with a proper burial mound.

(Penelope:) '[…] and now again a beloved son is gone on a hollow ship, an innocent all unversed in fighting and speaking, and it is for him I grieve even more than for that other one, and tremble for him and fear, lest something should happen to him either in the country where he has gone, or on the wide sea, for he has many who hate him and are contriving against him and striving to kill him before he comes back into his own country.' (4.817-823)

Thought: Penelope's concern for her son is touching. She loves and fears for him almost more than for Odysseus. The bond between mother and son is as strong as that between husband and wife in the *Odyssey*.

And as welcome as the show of life again in a father is to his children, when he has lain sick, suffering strong pains, and wasting long away, and the hateful death spirit has brushed him, but then, and it is welcome, the gods set him free of his sickness, so welcome appeared land and forest now to Odysseus, and he swam, pressing on, so as to set foot on the mainland. (5.394-399)

Thought: In this epic simile, Odysseus is made a child and his homeland his father; this familial motif is powerful in the *Odyssey*.

(Athene, disguised as the little girl:) 'So she was held high in the heart and still she is so, by her beloved children, by Alkinoös himself, and by the people, who look toward her as to a god when they see her, and speak in salutation as she walks about in her city. For there is no good intelligence that she herself lacks. She dissolves quarrels, even among men, when she favors them.' (7.69-74)

Thought: Queen Arete is so loved by her husband that she practically has as much ruling power as he does; her favor, not the king's, must be won by a guest for them to stay in the kingdom, and she settles legal matters with the same authority as her husband.

So the famous singer sang his tale, but Odysseus melted, and from under his eyes the tears ran down, drenching his cheeks. As a woman weeps, lying over the body of her dear husband, who fell fighting for her city and people as he tried to beat off the pitiless day from city and children; she sees him dying and gasping for breath, and winding her body about him she cries high and shrill, while the men behind her, hitting her with their spear butts on the back and the shoulders, force her up and lead her away into slavery, to have hard work and sorrow, and her cheeks are wracked with pitiful weeping. Such were the pitiful tears Odysseus shed from under his brows, but they went unnoticed by all the others […]. (8.521-532)

Thought: Yet another epic simile uses the familial motif to shows the depth Odysseus's emotion.

(Alkinoös:) 'Or could it then have been some companion, a brave man knowing thoughts gracious toward you, since one who is your companion, and has thoughts honorable toward you, is of no less degree than a brother?'

Thought: Alkinoös's remarks show that the ties of family aren't everything; ties of friendship can be even closer.

(Odysseus:) 'So I spoke, and my queenly mother answered me quickly: "All too much with enduring heart she does wait for you there in your own palace, and always with her the wretched nights and the days also waste her away with weeping. No one yet holds your fine inheritance, but in freedom Telemachos administers your allotted lands, and apportions the equal feasts, work that befits a man with authority to judge, for all to call him in. Your father remains, on the estate where he is, and does not go to the city. There is no bed there nor is there bed clothing nor blankets nor shining coverlets, but in the winter time he sleeps in the house, where the thralls do, in the dirt next to the fire, and with foul clothing upon him; but when the summer comes and the blossoming time of harvest, everywhere he has places to sleep on the ground, on fallen leaves in piles along the rising ground of his orchard, and there he lies, grieving, and the sorrow grows big within him as he longs for your homecoming, and harsh old age is on him. And so it was with me also and that was the reason I perished, nor in my palace did the lady of arrows, well-aiming, come upon me with her painless shafts, and destroy me, nor was I visited by sickness, which beyond other things takes the life out of the body with hateful weakness, but, shining Odysseus, it was my longing for you, your cleverness and your gentle ways, that took the sweet spirit of life from me.'* (11.180-203)

Thought: Through Antikleia's words, we see that an incomplete family becomes dysfunctional in the culture of the *Odyssey*.

(Odysseus, in his tale:) "Mother, why will you not wait for me, when I am trying to hold you, so that even in Hades' with our arms embracing we can both take the satisfaction of dismal mourning? Or are you nothing but an image that proud Persephone sent my way, to make me grieve all the more for sorrow?"* (11.210-214)

Thought: Odysseus is pained over the loss of his mother and the immediate futility of trying to take her "shade" in his arms; he is denied even the small comfort of human touch.

(Telemachos:) 'We went to Pylos, and to Nestor, shepherd of the people, and he, in his high house, gave me hospitality, and loving free attention, as a father would to his own beloved son, who was newly arrived from a long voyage elsewhere. So he freely took care of me, with his own glorious children.'* (17.109-113)

Thought: Telemachos himself is treated as family when in fact he is only a guest.

(Odysseus:) 'But now I shall go to our estate with its many orchards, to see my noble father who has grieved for me constantly.' (23.354-355)

Thought: Odysseus shows his devotion and duty to his family by immediately leaving to see his father after his emotional reunion with his wife.

He spoke, and the black cloud of sorrow closed on Laertes. In both hands he caught up the grimy dust and poured it over his face and grizzled head, groaning incessantly. The spirit rose up in Odysseus, and now in his nostrils there was a shock of bitter force as he looked on his father. He sprang to him and embraced and kissed him [...]. (24.315-319)

Thought: Laertes falls into the depths of despair when he thinks his son is still missing. Why would Odysseus play such a dirty trick on him?

Plot Analysis

Classic Plot Analysis

Initial Situation
Things are bad in Ithaka and Odysseus is still a captive on a distant island.
The residents of Odysseus's great hall are being eaten out of house and home by parasitic suitors who have no sense of propriety. Telemachos, Odysseus's son, has yet to prove his manhood. As for Odysseus himself, he is being held prisoner on the island of the nymph Kalypso – but nobody back in Ithaka knows that.

Conflict
Anchors aweigh!
The conflict stage begins when we finally see change from what has, for seven years or so, been the status quo. Much of this change has to do with divine intervention; Zeus sends his messenger to force Kalypso into letting Odysseus leave and Athene convinces Telemachos to go on his trip seeking news of his father. The conflict, then, is in Odysseus's struggle to return home and in Telemachos's search for his dad.

Complication
Odysseus makes a detour; Telemachos can't find him.
OK, so we all know Odysseus going straight home just isn't in the cards. As it happens, Poseidon whips up one more big storm to drive Odysseus onto the coast of the Phaiakians. In their court, he tells of all his adventures up to this point. Of course, the "complications" he tells about happened before the main epic begins – but, interestingly, Homer presents them at the time of the classic complication stage. In the meantime, Telemachos has been asking all the main Greek heroes, but hasn't been able to find his dad.

Climax
Odysseus arrives home in Ithaka.
When Odysseus arrives home, it represents the culmination of the initial phase of the story, in which he was wandering around looking for home. It will all be downhill from here. Have you ever tried running downhill? You think skiers have it easy? That's right, the homestretch is where you're likely to break your neck. As a result, the climax of the *Odyssey* only prepares us for the next stage…

Suspense
Disguised as a beggar, Odysseus infiltrates the palace.
This section of Homer's poem has all the classic elements of suspense. First of all, there's the underlying danger of Odysseus entering the palace, which is full of a whole bunch of suitors who have been acting like he's dead, and would to keep things that way – permanently. Then, of course, there are the many close-calls, where it looks like Odysseus is going to be revealed – like when Theoklymenos prophesies that he has returned; when Argos the dog recognizes him; when Odysseus talks to Penelope face-to-face; and when Eurykleia recognizes Odysseus's scar while giving him a foot-bath. The suspense reaches its highest level when Penelope proclaims the contest to the suitors: whoever can string Odysseus's bow and shoot an arrow through twelve axe heads can have her hand in marriage. Uh-oh, who's it gonna be?

Denouement
Odysseus kills the suitors and sleeps with Penelope.
By stringing the bow, winning the arrow-shooting contest, and killing the suitors (with a little help from Telemachos, Eumaios, Philoitios, and the goddess Athene), Odysseus takes care of the major problem facing him on the home front. That night, he goes to sleep with Penelope in their bed; the dramatic resolution is signaled by the fact that they tell stories about what has happened since they last saw each other.

Conclusion
Peace comes to Ithaka.
Fearing retribution from the families of the suitors, Odysseus and Telemachos go to the countryside to see Laertes. Odysseus and Laertes have a tearful reunion. When the families of the suitors come, Odysseus, Laertes, and Telemachos, along with some guys who work on Laertes's farm, arm for battle and face them down. They kill a few of them, but then Athene shouts out from the heavens and Zeus thunders. Everyone turns green with fear – and decides to let bygones be bygones. This ties up the last loose-end before Odysseus can…set off on his next journey (as prophesied by Teiresias in Book XI).

Booker's Seven Basic Plots Analysis: The Quest

The Call
None in the book, references to the Trojan War
This Booker Plot goes in chronological order, not in the order Homer tells the story. That's just the way it works; also, Booker practically built "The Quest" plot around the *Odyssey*, since Homer established some of the traditions of stories like this one. "The Call" is Odysseus's

yearning to go home from Troy once the city has been destroyed and the war is over. Along with the other Ithakans, our hero begins his journey home.

The Journey
Books V-XIII
While sailing, Odysseus faces obstacles like monsters (the Cyclops Polyphemos, Skylla and Charybdis) and temptations (the Lotus Eaters, the witch Circe, the Sirens, and Kalypso). Along the way, he receives advice from gods (Athene, Hermes), beautiful women (Circe, Kalypso), and wise old seers (Teiresias).

Arrival and Frustration
Books XIV-XVI
The Phaiakians bring Odysseus safely home to Ithaka, but Odysseus realizes that he must walk in disguise, find allies amidst the traitors, and plot against the suitors.

The Final Ordeals
Books XVII-XXII
In this stage, the hero undergoes a "series of tests" to prove he is worth his goal/prize/wife, etc. In this case, Odysseus has to prove first his patience (he can't beat the living pulp out of men like Antinoös, as that would give away his disguise), then his physical prowess (by winning Penelope's contest), his knowledge (with regards to the unmovable bed), and finally his diplomacy (by diffusing the angry-parents situation and restoring peace to Ithaka).

The Goal
Book XXIV
By defeating the suitors, Odysseus reclaims his faithful bride Penelope, his father in Laertes, his house, and is accepted by the Ithakan people as King.

Three Act Plot Analysis

Act I
The suitors are annoying Penelope in Ithaka and Telemachos, fed up, finally begins to speak out against them. He goes to the Grecian mainland to get news of his father from Odysseus's friends. Meanwhile, Odysseus has been stuck on Kalypso's island for seven years.

Act II
Odysseus escapes Kalypso's island with the help of the gods, is shipwrecked yet again, and floats to the island of Phaiákia where he is welcomed and urged to tell his story. He does.

Act III
Odysseus's story is over. Moved, the Phaiakians provide him with safe passage home. Once in Ithaka, he plots with Athene and Telemachos to kill the suitors. He eventually succeeds in a bloody battle, is reunited with Penelope, and brings peace to Ithaka once more.

Study Questions

1. What kinds of roles do women play in the *Odyssey*? Which females hold the most power and why?
2. How does the *Odyssey* define love? Why are Odysseus's affairs with Circe and Kalypso not considered true love?
3. What's up with the structure of the *Odyssey*? What is the effect of Homer starting *in media res* (in the middle of things)?
4. Is it possible for a modern reader to accept Odysseus's killing of the suitors? If not, how does this change in values affect our enjoyment of Homer's poem?
5. What is it about the *Odyssey* that makes it so timeless? What's so appealing that it's resulted in dozens and dozens of spin-offs?

Characters

All Characters

Odysseus Character Analysis

Odysseus is a Greek hero, King of Ithaka, son of Laertes, husband to Penelope, father of Telemachos, favorite of Athene, nemesis of Poseidon, and inventor of the Trojan horse. Odysseus's most dominant characteristic, besides his pecs, is his cunning. He is known for being the wiliest of the Greek heroes, and his wits save his life several times – most notably in the episode with the Cyclops. His mastery at improvisation, disguise, and dissembling help him hide his identity from potential enemies and scope out the loyalty of the person he is fooling. Though some modern sensibilities might question Odysseus's morality, because of his lying all the time – like pretending to be a Cretan, and deceiving his son and wife – he justifies these actions by their ends. His disguises and lies are usually sanctioned by Athene, his patron goddess, who also takes on many guises to manipulate humans and achieve her goals.

As for his pecs, well, let's just say that Odysseus can come off as *that guy* – what with all his ripping his shirt off in public, taunting the Cyclops after blinding him, and so on. The thing is that, even though Odysseus talks big, he *can* kick butt – at discus-throwing, verbal spars, bow-stringing, arrow-shooting, wandering the sea, being in disguise, confusing his opponents, and generally being The Man.

What gets Odysseus into trouble is when his justifiable pride shades into *hubris*, or arrogance. At worst, this can cloud Odysseus's better judgment – as when his not-so-tactful taunting of the

Cyclops sets off the whole feud between him and Poseidon. Because Odysseus just had to get the glory of besting the monster, he ended up wandering the sea for seventeen years and losing all of his companions to an untimely death.

That said, even if Odysseus's pride does sometimes get out of hand, his *hubris* doesn't even come close to that of the suitors, who trample on the laws of god and man by their violations of hospitality. Besides, Odysseus knows how to rein things in, as when he dresses up as a poor man to infiltrate the palace. Sure, he's still eager to prove his strength, but he manages, with Athene's help, to keep up appearances long enough to test the palace's inhabitants. This allows him to weed out the truly evil suitors from the decent ones – even though he does just kill them all in the end.

Odysseus's ruthlessness during this final slaughter can make us pause – especially when he has the maids slaughtered after forcing them to clean up all the blood-and-guts mess in the palace. "What happened to mercy or forgiveness?" we might ask. One of the things to remember while reading the *Odyssey* is that Greek values were different than ours. Justice may be blind, but she's also one tough cookie. (She carries a sword as well as those scales, remember?) In any case, Odysseus does spare the loyal maids, the singer, the town crier, and others that are loyal to him. And let's not forget, the whole poem *does* end with forgiveness – specifically when the families of the dead suitors are forced by the gods to forgive Odysseus and his family.

And while we're on the topic of cultural differences: if you start hating Odysseus for cheating on his wife left and right while she slept alone for two decades, just remember that there was a double-standard back in the day, like it or not. We're not supposed to see Odysseus as a jerk for this. We're supposed to think "It's not *his* fault these beautiful, immortal ladies can't keep their hands off him!"

Odysseus Timeline and Summary

- We learn that Poseidon hates Odysseus and that Athene is trying to help him.
- The gods reveal that Odysseus is at the moment stuck on Kalypso's island.
- Meanwhile, back in Ithaka, everyone thinks he's dead.
- We find out that, after the Trojan war, Odysseus stayed with King Agamemnon to try to appease the goddess Athene.
- Finally, after seven years, Zeus sends down Hermes to tell Kalypso to let Odysseus go; he sets out on a raft.
- Poseidon wrecks his raft, but the nereid Ino helps him get to shore.
- The shore turns out to be Scheria, where Odysseus is found by the princess Nausikaa. She brings him to court, where he begs mercy of the queen and is welcomed.
- King Alkinoös declares the next day a festal day in Odysseus's honor.
- Odysseus rocks in the athletic games. He just can't help himself.
- During the festivities, Odysseus hears stories of himself told by the bard and cries in sorrow.

- When King Alkinoös sees him crying, he asks him to identify himself and tell his story.
- Odysseus launches into the longest dinner party story ever:
- After leaving from Troy, Odysseus and his crew land in the city of Ismaros and raid it for no good reason. The next day, the people retaliate with a late-arriving cavalry and kill many of Odysseus's men.
- Odysseus and his men suffer through three days of intense storms.
- Ten days later, they land on the island of the Lotus Eaters. Odysseus explores the land with a scouting party. When he discovers that they lose their memory and all their will to go home after eating the lotus flower, he forces them all back to the ship as fast as he can and sails away.
- They next arrive at the land of the Cyclopes, giants with only one eye, where Odysseus makes the mistake of not getting out as quickly as he can. Instead he wants to talk to Polyphemos.
- Polyphemos traps the Ithakans in his cave and eats a few men.
- Odysseus tells Polyphemos his name is "Nobody" and offers him enough wine to get him seriously drunk.
- Odysseus blinds Polyphemos with a sharpened stake thrust into his eye as the Cyclops sleeps, drunk.
- Odysseus laughs at Polyphemos when he calls for help; he tells his friends that "Nobody" is hurting him, which is a great way to not obtain help from your buddies.
- Odysseus ties his men under the sheep so that they escape the next morning when the blinded Cyclops lets his flocks out to graze.
- Odysseus taunts Polyphemos from his ship and reveals his true name and destination. Not a good decision.
- Polyphemos calls down the wrath of his father Poseidon on Odysseus. He curses the man and hopes he loses all his companions and is generally miserable. Forever.
- Next, the men land on Aiolia, where the god of the winds (Aiolos) plays host to them for a month before giving Odysseus a farewell gift: a bag of storm winds to blow his ship home safely.
- Unfortunately, Odysseus jealously guards the secret of what's inside the bag so when he falls asleep, his men, thinking the sack contains a treasure open it and let the winds escape.
- The ship, just as it's coming in sight of Ithaka, is blown back towards Aiolia. Aiolos refuses to help them, saying that Odysseus must be cursed by the gods.
- Odysseus and his men sail until they reach Lamos. There, they are taken by the princess to the king, who promptly eats one of Odysseus's men. The rest of them escape, totally freaked out.
- The Ithakans then sail to Aiaia, island of the witch Circe, where Odysseus's men are lured into her home and turned into pigs.
- With Hermes's help and a magical herb, Odysseus resists being turned into an animal and manages to get Circe to promise that she won't use anymore magic on him. She does, so he sleeps with her (which is a nice reward for not doing magic).
- They all stay with the witch for a year until one of the Ithakans reminds Odysseus that, hey, they're sort of on a mission to get home here.
- Once everyone's ready to leave, Circe tells Odysseus he must visit the seer Teiresias in the Underworld.
- Odysseus does not notice one of his men, Elpenor, fall off the roof and die, since he's too

busy loading up his ship.

- In the Underworld, Odysseus makes blood sacrifices as commanded and talks to the shades.
- Teiresias advises him not to eat any of Helios's cattle on Thrinakia. He also tells Odysseus how to ensure himself a peaceful death.
- Then Odysseus speaks to the shades of many famous dead princesses and heroes.
- This is the one moment where Odysseus pulls out of his story and talks again to the Phaiakians. Of course, he shortly goes back to his tale:
- Once out of the Underworld, Odysseus makes a funeral pyre for Elpenor as the man's ghost requested in the Underworld.
- Circe comes back and advises Odysseus on how to get past the Sirens as well as Skylla and Charybdis, all of which he has to pass to get home.
- After doing so, the men have lost many of their friends and are shaken. They vote to stay on the island of Thrinakia, despite Odysseus's desire to go onward.
- The Ithakans are stranded for a month due to storms.
- Starving, the men – led by Eurylochos – decide to kill and eat Helios' cattle.
- When they next sail, Zeus strikes them down with a thunderbolt, destroying Odysseus's ship and killing everyone but our hero.
- After escaping Skylla and Charybdis for a second time, Odysseus drifts for nine days until he washes ashore on Kalypso's island.
- There he is seduced and trapped for seven years by the enraptured nymph Kalypso, although he chooses not to go into details and ends his story.
- The Phaiakians are so moved by Odysseus's story that they offer his safe passage home.
- When Odysseus wakes up in Ithaka, Athene reveals herself to him and they make plans to defeat the suitors.
- Odysseus, dressed as a beggar, goes to the forest home of his swineherd Eumaios and crashes on his couch.
- Shortly thereafter, having been advised by Athene, Telemachos shows up. Odysseus reveals his true identity to his son and together they plan to defeat the soldiers.
- Odysseus comes to town disguised as a beggar and, well, begs in the great hall, his own home, to find out which suitors are decent men and which are wicked.
- Antinoös throws a stool at him. (He goes on the "wicked" list.)
- Odysseus gets into a fight with Iros, another tramp, and defeats him easily.
- Still disguised, Odysseus speaks with Penelope. She welcomes him as a friend when he convinces her that he housed Odysseus, but she still doesn't believe that her husband is alive.
- The nurse Eurykleia sees through the beggar disguise when she washes his feet and uncovers an old hunting scar. He swears her to secrecy.
- As the suitors are preoccupied with his bow, Odysseus approaches his two shepherds and asks if they would be loyal to their master if he returned. When they answer affirmatively, he reveals himself and enlists them as fighters in the upcoming battle.
- Odysseus, still disguised as a beggar, wins Penelope's contest by stringing his own massive bow and shooting an arrow through the twelve axe heads.
- He and Telemachos, along with the loyal herdsmen, kill all the suitors in the great hall.
- Afterwards, Odysseus forces all the disloyal maids to clean up the slaughter and then has them killed as well. Best to not leave any loose, treacherous ends.
- Odysseus wins back Penelope by revealing their "secret" to her – the fact that their bed is

carved from the roots of an olive tree and is therefore immovable.

- The reunited couple spends the night together.
- The next day, Odysseus visits his father Laertes and reveals himself to him. There is much rejoicing.
- A group of Ithaka rebels shows up; they want revenge for their murdered sons (the suitors).
- They fight.
- Athene makes them stop fighting.
- Eventually, the people and Odysseus form a pact. Restored to his kingship, Odysseus brings peace to Ithaka once more.

Telemachos Character Analysis

Telemachos is the son of Odysseus and Penelope. He is marked by his prudence and, as we are told time and again, his clear-headedness. This guy is not one to rush into action without first considering the consequences. That said, he *is* getting impatient with all these suitors, who are wasting his family's riches, treating him badly, and trying to snag (and snog) his mother. What this means is that we pick up the action at the most exciting part – when Telemachos is finally about to do something about it.

It's notable that it takes a good deal of coaxing from Athene to goad Telemachos into action. The young man repeatedly refers to the fact that the suitors are older, stronger, more experienced, and likely better fighters than he is. (This makes sense; Penelope at one point references him growing a beard for the first time, so he's just maturing when the story starts.) One major theme in the *Odyssey*, therefore, is Telemachos's physical, emotional, and spiritual growth.

Part of the way we trace this growth is by watching Telemachos's interactions with his mother. One way he asserts his adult status is by telling her what to do – thereby taking control of their relationship. Penelope, far from being bothered, encourages this behavior, clearly glad to see her son stepping up to his role. Another is when he leaves on his journey without telling her in advance. (Penelope is less pleased about this.)

All the same, it's a lot easier to stand up to his mother than it is to give the suitors what's coming to them. After all, even public speaking gives this guy the shakes. This is one reason why Telemachos is so eager to find his father – for help. When Odysseus comes, Telemachos suddenly gains confidence – notice how he insults the suitors more and more freely? Suddenly, he is able to fight, even despite his lack of combat experience. Not that he's an expert. When he screws up by forgetting to close the door to the room where he's hid the suitors' weapons, we can see that he still has a lot to learn.

That said, the poem gives us confidence that we will get there. A lot of this has to do with genetics; after all, he is Odysseus's son. Telemachos's ability to string the bow (Homer says he was about to do it before Odysseus gave him the signal to knock it off) is certainly a mark of his innate (and likely inherited) strength. Again, because of his paternity, Telemachos is

sheltered and protected by Athene – Odysseus's own private support system and powerful lucky charm. It is appropriate, then, that in the retribution scene we see Telemachos side-by-side with his father and grandfather, dispensing justice as one, united front.

Telemachos Timeline and Summary

- Telemachos greets Athene, who comes to Odysseus's home disguised as Mentor. He apologizes for the suitors' rough behavior.
- Athene advises Telemachos to go to Sparta and ask for news about Odysseus from Nestor and Menelaos.
- Telemachos issues an ultimatum to the suitors: they must be gone at dawn. He is laughed at and can't really do anything about the situation. Other than pout.
- Telemachos calls a meeting of the Ithakan men. He shames the suitors and calls the general public out for not speaking out against them.
- Telemachos leaves that night for Pylos. There, he learns from Nestor that Odysseus is a great favorite of Athene's and hears the story of Orestes, whom he admires for doing what was necessary to clear his family name.
- Telemachos leaves for Sparta to see King Menelaos.
- Menelaos recognizes Telemachos as Odysseus's son and tells him stories of Odysseus during the Trojan War. Telemachos is told that Odysseus is still alive – and stuck on Kalypso's island.
- A few days later, although it's been about eight years for us as we've been listening to Odysseus's story, Telemachos, still in Sparta, is approached by Athene and told to come home. Right now.
- He does, even bypassing Nestor's hospitality, which we've seen can drag on for quite some time.
- Just as he is about to pull out of port, Telemachos is approached by a stranger named Theoklymenos, a seer and a fugitive begging passage aboard his ship. Telemachos grants it. He's a nice guy.
- Athene guides Telemachos's ship away from the suitors' ambush.
- Telemachos, following Athene's instructions, goes to Eumaios's hut, where he meets Odysseus in beggar form.
- At Athene's orders, Odysseus reveals his true self to his son. There is much rejoicing. Then they start plotting to slaughter all the suitors.
- Telemachos goes back to town to see his mother and orders Eumaios to bring Odysseus along later.
- Penelope questions Telemachos about what he learned of Odysseus on his journey. He tells his mother the truth, but not the whole truth. (He omits the little fact that Odysseus is in fact already home.)
- Telemachos vows his protection to the beggar in front of all the suitors at dinner.
- Penelope comes downstairs to scold Telemachos about letting the beggar suffer abuse at her table while all the suitors go crazy with lust at the sight of her.
- That night, Telemachos and Odysseus move the suitors' weapons out of the great hall and into a locked storage room.

- Telemachos is the first to try the string-the-bow test. He almost succeeds on his fourth attempt, but is stopped by Odysseus's signal.
- Telemachos fights alongside Odysseus against the suitors and kills his first men.
- He carelessly leaves the storage room door open when getting weapons, which allows Melanthios to arm the suitors. Telemachos confesses his fault to Odysseus.
- Telemachos speaks on behalf of Phemios and Medon – both loyal servants of the household – and Odysseus refrains from killing them.
- When Odysseus orders that the disloyal maids be killed by sword, Telemachos instead hangs them so as to render their death more dishonorable.
- Telemachos goes with Odysseus and the herdsmen the next day to see Laertes.
- When the Ithakan rebels show up, Telemachos invokes Athene and kills the ringleader, Eupeithes. This eventually leads to peace.

Penelope Character Analysis

Penelope is the wife of Odysseus, mother of Telemachos, Queen of Ithaka, and the object of desire for every nobleman in the land. She's also a strong woman. This may seem like crazy-talk by today's standards (after all, she lets her son boss her around and seems pleased at his behavior), but this is ancient Greece. Look at how she holds out against the suitors. Surely it would have been easier simply to marry one of them and get the whole mess over with, but Penelope sticks to her guns. Most importantly, she does this through cunning and deception – just look at her brilliant ruse about weaving a shroud for Laertes – which makes her a pretty good match for our crafty hero Odysseus.

Penelope's decision not to re-marry demonstrates her fortitude and determination. At the same time, it makes her the shining example of faithfulness and fidelity in the *Odyssey*. Despite her long suffering and yearning for her husband, she sleeps alone for nearly twenty years (unlike her husband, we might add). Homer really drives home Penelope's suffering throughout all this: we see her crying into her pillow each night, longing for Odysseus.

Whether or not Penelope thinks her husband is dead is an interesting question. She's certainly skeptical anytime someone claims he is alive, or present. But just because she's skeptical doesn't mean she's lost faith. Right up to the last moment, Penelope lets her mind do double-duty, holding faith and doubt in balance. If anything, this makes her fidelity all the more impressive (and perhaps even more impressive than Odysseus's rejection of the immortality offered by Kalypso): without the certainty that Odysseus would one day come home, she risked being alone until her death.

Penelope Timeline and Summary

- For three years, Penelope has put off choosing a husband among the suitors by saying that she must first finish weaving a shroud for Laertes. Each day she weaves and each

night she unravels her day's work. Thus she delays for three years until a treacherous maid spills the beans.

- Penelope is forced to complete the shroud and now has no more excuses to continue delaying her choice.
- Penelope comes down from her room during a banquet to request that the singer sing a song – not one about the Trojan war – because it saddens her to listen. Her son scolds her, so she goes back upstairs.
- The town crier brings Penelope news that her son has sailed to Pylos and that the suitors are planning to ambush and kill him when he comes back.
- Penelope prays to Athene to bring her son home safely.
- Athene sends Penelope a dream of her sister, Iphthime, who tells her that Telemachos will come home safely by the will of the gods.
- Penelope asks her for information about her husband, but is denied.
- Several days later, Eumaios the swineherd arrives with the information that Telemachos has returned home safely. As instructed by Odysseus, he whispers the news to Penelope so that no one else will hear.
- Simultaneously, a runner comes bearing the same news. Unfortunately, he shouts it from the rooftops, so there goes the whole "discreet" thing.
- Penelope asks her son twice about news regarding Odysseus and gets information on her second try.
- She feels a small seed of hope stirring within her at the news that Odysseus was seen alive not long ago, but she conceals her optimism.
- Penelope is told by Theoklymenos that Odysseus is already on the island, much to Telemachos's chagrin. But she doesn't believe him.
- As Antinoös causes trouble for the beggar in the great hall below, Penelope hears and tells her maid to send the man up to her for questioning.
- Eumaios returns with a message to the frantic Penelope that the beggar will come up later tonight when the suitors are asleep. Penelope realizes this is prudent.
- Penelope, feeling frisky under the influence of Athene, goes down to scold her son while standing promiscuously in front of the suitors.
- The suitors are stunned by her superhuman beauty, thanks to Athene. Each lusts after her and vows to win her for himself.
- Penelope flirtily laments to her suitors that none of them have courted her properly. She wants gifts, which they scramble to bring her. Odysseus, watching, is amused, in a "my wife's still got it" kind of way.
- Penelope meets the beggar up in her room that night and asks for information regarding her husband.
- Odysseus, disguised as the beggar, gives her false information. He says he has hosted Odysseus recently and that the man is indeed on his way home.
- The Queen does not believe him, so she asks for details of Odysseus's appearance, which the beggar flawlessly provides.
- Penelope is overcome with emotion and welcomes the beggar as a friend.
- After Penelope orders a foot bath for her guest (where Eurykleia discovers the true identity of the beggar), she asks him to interpret a dream for her. In it, an eagle kills and scatters her flock of farm geese.
- Actually, the eagle then explains that he represents Odysseus and the geese represent the suitors, but still, Penelope is somehow at a loss.

- So beggar Odysseus reaffirms the eagle's claim.
- Penelope remains unconvinced.
- The Queen decides to wait no longer. She issues a contest the next day in which the winner will be the man to string Odysseus's old bow and shoot an arrow through twelve axe heads. She promises to marry the suitor who wins.
- Penelope scolds Antinoös for trying to scare the beggar away from competing.
- Telemachos tells Penelope to go upstairs because this is a man's affair and obviously no concern of a woman, since it's not taking place in the bedroom. She obeys. Chick power yet again.
- After the slaughter, Eurykleia comes to Penelope with the news that Odysseus is back and has killed all the suitors. Penelope does not believe her.
- Penelope remains skeptical even when she sees her husband standing before her. She insists that the real Odysseus would know their secret sign.
- Penelope is only convinced after she tricks Odysseus into revealing their secret – the fact that their marriage bed is carved straight from live olive roots and cannot be moved.
- She welcomes him back tearfully.
- The happy couple spends a blissful night together where they make love and exchange stories of the twenty long years.
- The next morning, as Odysseus goes off to visit his father, he orders Penelope to lock herself and all the women upstairs to keep them safe from any townspeople who want to avenge the murders of the suitors.

Athene Character Analysis

The daughter of Zeus, Athene is the goddess of wisdom and patroness of warfare. This combination makes it come as no surprise that she likes a hero with some brains in him – namely Odysseus. That's why she helps him do everything from winning favors to devising plans to not dying to looking sexy. Athene also parallels Odysseus in her fondness for disguises, ranging from an elderly Ithakan to a beggar to the resident prince. To really drive the point home, the very last line of the poem tells how the dispute between Odysseus and the families of the dead suitors was settled by Athene, "who had likened herself in appearance and voice to Mentor."

Why does Athene like playing dress-up so much? Even though we at Shmoop shudder at claiming to know the will of the gods, we have a few ideas. Number one: because it's fun and because she can. Number two: it's a way of testing mortals, to see if they treat her well when she's disguised as one of them. Number three: it lets her keep a low profile. That way, when you bust out by shining your divine aegis through the air, people know you mean business.

And does she ever mean business. Just look at how often Athene is able to get her own way, even in her interactions with the other gods. When she asks that Zeus command Circe to let Odysseus go, he delays but eventually does comply with his daughter's request. Heck, if you're looking for a female-power heroine, Athene might even beat out Penelope. (Though the contest *is* a little unfair, Athene being a goddess and all.) But the moment where we really see

Athene bust out the big guns is in the last third of the epic. Here is where she really becomes the incarnation of divine justice, spurring Odysseus on to kill the suitors – all the suitors. We were all a little surprised to see that Amphinomos met the same unfortunate end as the rest of the crew, and even more surprised to see that Athene, who until now seemed perfectly reasonable, was the one clamoring for his death. What gives?

The goddess is clearly out for blood, but we should try not to read this as evidence that Athene is violence-crazed and unfair. She just has an austere sense of justice, which back in the day was the way justice worked. Just look at Telemachos's post-slaughter insistence on hanging the maids, so as to give them the least honorable death possible. The characters believe this is the way justice is served: with a lengthy sword.

One more thing. While, Athene's interest in helping Odysseus does have a lot to do with their similar personas, it's also possible that Athene's not-so-positive relationship with Poseidon might play a role. Even though Athene and Poseidon were allied against the Trojans during the Trojan War, they also have a history of conflict with each other. One traditional story traced this to a debate over who got to be the patron of Athens. (Clearly, you can see who won *that* argument.) This tradition isn't explicitly referenced in the *Odyssey* itself, but it might have formed part of the background info that early Greek audiences would have taken for granted.

Athene Timeline and Summary

- Up on Mount Olympos, Zeus discusses the recent and just murder of Klytaimestra and her lover Aigisthos by Orestes.
- Athene replies and turns her father's thoughts toward Odysseus, stranded at sea. She asks for his mercy, and Zeus reassures her.
- Disguised as Mentor, Athene goes down to Odysseus's house and advises Telemachos to go to Pylos and Sparta to find out information about his father.
- When Telemachos's meeting with the Ithakans fails, he prays to Athene for help.
- She hears him and answers, ordering him prepare for a journey and promising to secure a ship for his travels.
- Disguised as Telemachos, Athene rents a ship from Noëmon.
- Disguised as Mentor, Athene and Telemachos and his crew head for Pylos.
- After being urged by pious Peisistratos to make an offering to Poseidon, Athene – highly amused – does. Then, she grants each of her prayers for them herself.
- When Nestor offers Telemachos and Mentor/Athene a bed for the night, Athene refuses graciously. As she leaves, she creates a sign to reveal her divine presence.
- Nestor promises to make ritual sacrifices for her the next day and follows through.
- That same night, Athene comes to the distressed Penelope in a dream, disguised as her sister Iphthime, and tells Penelope that her son will come home safely, as the gods will it.
- Athene begs Zeus to let Odysseus leave the island of Kalypso. He agrees.
- When Poseidon sends a storm to delay Odysseus on his raft, Athene calms the winds and drifts Odysseus towards Scheria where he will find help from the Phaiakian people.
- Athene goes to the Phaiakian princess Nausikaa in her dreams and, as a friend, advises

her to prepare for marriage by washing her linens in the streams.

- Nausikaa goes down to the streams the next day where she meets the stranded and desperate Odysseus; she promises to help him.
- Athene plays up his manly beauty and Nausikaa falls right into her hands by getting the hots for the Greek hero.
- Athene disguises herself as a little Phaiakian girl; she leads Odysseus towards the palace of King Alkinoös and tells him the history of the land. She advises him to entreaty Queen Arete for help, just as Nausikaa advised earlier.
- The next day, after Odysseus has secured safe passage home, Athene disguises herself as the town crier and brings all the Phaiakians to the palace with the news of the stranger's arrival.
- Once Odysseus is conveyed back to Ithaka and left sleeping on the shore, Athene hides him in a protective cloud so nobody can see him or his treasure as he sleeps.
- Athene approaches Odysseus disguised as a little girl and tells him he is in Ithaka. Duh.
- Then she reveals herself to Odysseus.
- Athene tells him she will disguise him as a beggar and that he must go to Eumaios's home in the forest. She transforms him into a beggar. Odysseus goes.
- Meanwhile, Athene flies to Sparta to tell Telemachos to come home immediately. She adds that he needs to come to Eumaios's hut as soon as he reaches Ithaka. Telemachos obeys.
- Athene guides Telemachos's ship safely away from the site of the suitors' planned ambush.
- At Eumaios's place, Athene tells Odysseus to reveal himself to his son; she then removes his disguise, which we have to say doesn't leave him with much choice anyway. Telemachos is stunned and overjoyed.
- Athene puts the disguise back on Odysseus when Eumaios returns to the hut, having delivered the news to Penelope that Telemachos is home safely.
- Athene makes Penelope even more beautiful and compels her to tease the suitors to arouse their lust. She succeeds.
- Athene holds a torch to light the way while Odysseus and Telemachos move the suitors' weapons from the great hall into a storage room.
- Before the test of the bow, Athene makes everything seem particularly funny to the suitors so they don't notice any strange preparations going on. Also, their teasing helps to inflame Odysseus and Telemachos's fury.
- During the slaughter, Athene arrives in the guise of Mentor and is implored by both sides to help them. She speaks in Odysseus's favor but does not actually fight for him yet. She waits for father and son to prove themselves worthy of her aid.
- She protects the four friends from the spears of the suitors.
- When Athene's sign shines on Odysseus's side, the suitors panic. Odysseus finishes killing them.
- When Penelope finally accepts Odysseus back, Athene slows down time so they can have all the time they need together.
- When Odysseus and company go off to see Laertes, she hides and protects them in a dark cloud.
- When Laertes welcomes Odysseus home, Athene makes him look years younger.
- When the Ithakan rebels come, Telemachos invokes Athene before throwing his spear and, sure enough, she aids him; the spear rips straight through the helmet of Eupeithes,

the lead rebel.

- Athene orders them all to stop fighting and make peace.
- They eventually do and Athene witnesses the pact, legitimizing Odysseus as King of Ithaka.

Antinoös Character Analysis

Antinoös is the human face we get to put to the otherwise nameless group of evil suitors. As such, Antinoös represents unbecoming greed and impropriety. He eats, drinks, raids Odysseus's supply of food and has no sense of restraint or respect for the King's house and name. This shows that he, and as an extension, the rest of the suitors, abuse their role as guests in Odysseus's house and show disrespect to their hostess (whose hand, ironically, they are trying to win). Thus they disregard the Greek value of hospitality, and in doing so, show themselves as something sub-human. Remember, we've seen throughout the course of the *Odyssey* that hospitality is a BIG DEAL in ancient Greece. Because it was held as one of Zeus's personal rules for the mortals, breaking the law of hospitality is impious and even sacrilegious.

Antinoös's lack of civility comes to light in certain key moments: when he tries to make beggar Odysseus fight with beggar Iros, when he throws a footstool at the beggar, and oh, yes, did we mention plotting to kill the Prince, his very host? Not cool, Antinoös. It's no surprise that, given the incredible importance of hospitality and the incredible degree to which the suitors deny it, Athene wants ALL the suitors to die, die, die.

To top it all off, Antinoös is lazy. He is the first to suggest that the suitors should eat and drink whenever they are playing sports or resting. He is the most pig-like of the bunch, gorging himself silly and constantly getting drunk. The most apparent instance of his laziness occurs when the men are trying to string Odysseus's bow. Seeing that the others have not come close to succeeding, Antinoös calls for them to stop and come eat; they will leave the bow for the morrow. It is appropriate that Antinoös is distracted with drinking wine when Odysseus puts an arrow through his throat.

Antinoös Timeline and Summary

- When Telemachos orders that the suitors leave by dawn, Antinoös protests and mocks Telemachos.
- During the Ithakan council, Antinoös condemns Telemachos for saying such shameful things about the suitors.
- He accuses Penelope herself of deceiving them all. He tells the story of Laertes's shroud.
- Antinoös issues an ultimatum to Telemachos: he must either banish Penelope or force her to choose a suitor. Telemachos refuses to do either.
- Antinoös learns from Noëmon that Telemachos went to Pylos instead of inland as he

claimed. Enraged, he suggests that the suitors ambush the young Prince on his way back and kill him. Everyone thinks this sounds just dandy.

- A few days later, when news that Telemachos has returned home safely reaches the suitors, Antinoös urges his fellow men to strike the first blow, now that it is common knowledge that they tried to kill the Prince.
- When the beggar first comes to the great hall during supper, Antinoös scolds Eumaios for bringing him.
- Antinoös, enraged at the beggar, throws a footstool at the man and hits him in the shoulder. Odysseus (the beggar) pretends to ignore it, but is seething inside.
- Antinoös urges the beggar and Iros to fight.
- During the test of the bow, Antinoös orders Melanthios to build a fire so that they can limber the bow over it in hopes of bending it (and therefore stringing it) more easily.
- This doesn't work.
- Antinoös, fearing that he will soon fail, suggests to his friends that they feast and try the bow thing tomorrow. So they feast.
- When the beggar asks to have a crack at the bow, Antinoös reprimands him for his daring; he (Antinoös) is overruled by Telemachos and the Queen.
- As Antinoös is raising a goblet of wine to his mouth, Odysseus kills him with an arrow to this throat.
- Antinoös dies.

Agamemnon Character Analysis

Brother of Menelaos and a Greek King. He was married to the unfaithful Klytaimestra and killed upon his return from Troy by her and her lover, Aigisthos. See "Symbols, Imagery, Allegory" for more.

Agelaos Character Analysis

Sometimes spelled Agelaus. One of the suitors we see in Book XXI. He asks Telemachos to reason with Penelope about marrying someone already.

Telamonian Aias Character Analysis

Sometimes spelled Ajax. A Greek hero in the Trojan war whom Odysseus encounters in the Underworld. Aias killed himself after Odysseus was named a greater man than he, and still refuses to speak to his friend even after death.

Little Aias Character Analysis

Sometimes spelled Ajax. A Greek who fought in the Trojan war, and also an irreverent jerk who raped and killed a princess on Athene's altar and was killed for his action.

Aigisthos Character Analysis

Sometimes spelled Aegisthus. The treacherous lover of Agamemnon's wife, Klytaimestra. He conspired with her to kill her husband and was later murdered in revenge by Orestes, Agamemnon's son.

Aigyptios Character Analysis

An Ithakan lord present at Telemachos's meeting in Book II.

Aiolos Character Analysis

Sometimes spelled Aeolus, Eolus or Aeolos. God of the winds; he helps Odysseus and his men in Book X, before he realizes there is no hope for the Ithakans.

Aithon Character Analysis

The fake name that Odysseus gives when speaking with Penelope while in the guise of a beggar. The scholar Olga Levaniouk has recently argued that this name means "fiery," in the sense of burning with desire or hunger. In this way, by telling Penelope this name, Odysseus is making a sneaky reference to his status as a beggar—as well as his burning desire to get his own life back, by kicking some serious butt.

Achilleus Character Analysis

Sometimes spelled Achilles. A big Greek hero that fought against the Trojans. He's already dead by the time the *Odyssey* begins, so we only see him in the Underworld. It is interesting that in the *Iliad* we hear Achilleus was given a choice: live a long and uneventful life, or get lots of glory and then die. Obviously, he chose the latter, but when we hear him speak as a "shade" it looks like he regrets it. He says he would rather live in the real world as the lowliest slave than be Big Man in Dead People Land.

Alkinoös Character Analysis

Sometimes spelled Alcinous. King of the Phaiakians, husband of Arete, father to Nausikaa. He's the guy who asks Odysseus to tell his story.

Amphimedon Character Analysis

One of the suitors. In the Underworld, he tells the story of the slaughter to Achilleus and Agamemnon. It's clear from his version that the suitors are none-too-repentant of their ways.

Amphinomos Character Analysis

Sometimes spelled Amphinomus. The good suitor, relatively speaking. Penelope seems to recognize this, as does Odysseus; he even goes so far as to warn Amphinomos to get out before the slaughter. Unfortunately, Athene wants everyone to die. So that's that.

Antikleia Character Analysis

Odysseus's mother; he converses with her in the Underworld and discovers that she has taken her own life out of grief for his continued absence.

Antilochos Character Analysis

Sometimes spelled Antilochus. One of Odysseus's war buddies with whom he converses in the Underworld. When alive, he was a good friend of Achilleus.

Antiphates Character Analysis

King of Lamos, the land of the not-so-human Laistrygones. He greets the Ithakans by attacking the first man he sees and drinking his blood.

Antiphos Character Analysis

Sometimes spelled Antiphus. One of the Ithakan men. He remains loyal to Odysseus; Telemachos consults with him among others in Book XVII.

Aphrodite Character Analysis

Goddess of love. In the land of the Phaiakians, the bard Demodokos sings a tale about Aphrodite cheating on her husband (Hephaistos) with the God of war (Ares); she is caught in the act, literally, when her husband catches the lovers in a net and lets everyone have a look-see.

Ares Character Analysis

God of war. He is referenced in the *Odyssey* as the lover of Aphrodite, who was married. He and Aphrodite were caught – during sex – by her husband Hephaistos, and shown to the world while wearing his birthday suit.

Arete Character Analysis

Queen of the Phaiakians, wife to Alkinoös, and mother to Nausikaa. She's the dominant one in her marriage, so Odysseus has to get her to like him in order to obtain help from her husband and her people. Arete is also a clever woman, as she figures out from Odysseus's clothing that Nausikaa has already helped him. Her name means "excellence."

Argos Character Analysis

Odysseus's loyal dog. When his master return homes after nearly twenty years, Argos recognizes him, rejoices, and dies. If you think Penelope had to wait a long time to see Odysseus again, try thinking of those twenty years in dog years!

Autolykos Character Analysis

Sometimes spelled Autolycus. Odysseus's maternal grandfather. We only hear about him in a flashback; he's the one Odysseus was hunting with as a boy when he got the tell-tale scar on his thigh that later reveals him to Eurykleia.

Kassandra Character Analysis

Sometimes spelled Cassandra. A Trojan princess. She was raped and killed by Little Aias on the altar of Athene, which meant he had to die for his disrespect. (The problem was the location more than the rape and murder, which is odd.)

Demodokos Character Analysis

Sometimes spelled Demodocus. The blind bard of the Phaiakians; has been traditionally thought (without any real basis) to be a representation of Homer himself. This is why we think Homer is blind. Demodokos sings about Achilleus and Odysseus (oblivious that one of those men is present), and later of Aphrodite.

Dolios Character Analysis

Laertes's housekeeper.

Eidothea Character Analysis

A nymph who comes into play in Menelaos's story to Telemachos about that one time he was stranded on an island. It was Eidothea who advised him to capture Proteus, the god of the island, to discern how to escape.

Elpenor Character Analysis

One of the Ithakans unfortunate enough to be traveling with Odysseus, and even more unfortunate to have wandered up to Circe's roof and fallen to his death before the men departed. Odysseus converses with him in the underworld, where Elpenor asks for a proper burial; this character reminds us of the importance of such matters (like proper burials, even if it means your crew has to sail back to the island of a sorceress to do so).

Eperitos Character Analysis

The name that Odysseus gives to his father, Laertes, in Book XXIV, before revealing his true identity.

Eumaios Character Analysis

Sometimes spelled Eumaeus. The Ithakan swineherd who takes Odysseus in when he returns home in the guise of a beggar. He provides an excellent example of hospitality.

Eupeithes Character Analysis

Antinoös's father. We meet him post-slaughter, while he's looking for a little vengeful slaughter

action himself – against Odysseus and Telemachos.

Eurykleia Character Analysis

Odysseus's nurse when he was a little boy. She's still around in the palace working as a servant when Odysseus returns and she recognizes her master by the scar on his thigh.

Eurylochos Character Analysis

Sometimes spelled Eurylochus. One of the Ithakans traveling with Odysseus on the way back from Troy. He is a cautious man, refusing to enter Circe's hall even when accompanied by armed men. He's also the brilliant mind who convinces everyone to stay a night at Thrinakia – land of Helios's cattle – which we all know results in the death of…everyone. Except Odysseus.

Eurymachos Character Analysis

Sometimes spelled Eurymachus. One of the not-so-nice suitors. He even plots to kill Telemachos and then deceives Penelope about it.

Halitherses Character Analysis

An Ithakan augur and loyal to Odysseus. In Book II, he interprets the two vicious eagles as a sign that Odysseus is coming home soon.

Helen Character Analysis

Menelaos's wife and instigator of the entire Trojan war. Although we don't hear this tale in the *Odyssey*, the following would have been common knowledge among Homer's audience. Here's the deal: Helen was the most beautiful woman ever. Seriously. She was married to a Greek king named Menelaos, which as far as we know was going swimmingly until Paris, the most handsome Trojan guy ever, decided he wanted her. (Actually, he settled a contest between three catty Goddesses and "won" her, but that's another story). So he stole Helen. And the Greeks launched a war against Troy, with many ships, swords, spears, arrows, and deaths. Then Menelaos got his wife back. In the *Odyssey*, we meet Helen when Telemachos visits Sparta for news of his father. She's very gracious, telling him stories of Odysseus and doing a good job of not starting any wars throughout the entire dinner conversation. (This might be helped by the fact that she drugs everyone's drinks.)

Helios Character Analysis

God of the sun. You might be wondering what's up with all this cattle – basically, Helios was famous not only for controlling the most essential body of matter in our solar system, but also for having some really awesome cattle that no one was allowed to touch, much less kill and eat. This is why Odysseus's men's doing just that was a big problem, and by "big" we mean "punishable by death."

Hephaistos Character Analysis

Sometimes spelled Hephæstos. Aphrodite's crippled blacksmith husband. Luckily, he married a beautiful goddess. Unluckily, she cheats.

Hermes Character Analysis

The messenger of the Gods. He doesn't seem to have any real personality of his own, but he sure is Zeus's yes-man.

Iphitos Character Analysis

A minor character in the story of How Odysseus Got His Bow. Actually, Iphitos is the man who gave him the bow.

Iphthime Character Analysis

Penelope's sister. She isn't actually present in the *Odyssey*, but in Book IV Athene sends a vision of her to Penelope in her sleep, to reassure the Queen that her husband is soon coming home.

Iros Character Analysis

Sometimes spelled Irus. Also known as Arnaeus. The real beggar of the palace in Ithaka. He gets territorial when a new beggar (who we know to be Odysseus in disguise) starts poking around his turf. Possibly one of the most hilarious scenes in the *Odyssey* comes when Iros challenges Odysseus to a fight, and the hero responds by ripping off his shirt and terrifying his opponent.

Kalypso Character Analysis

Sometimes spelled Calypso. The goddess who holds Odysseus hostage for purposes of sex.

Charybdis Character Analysis

Monster #2 of the worst duo ever. Skylla and Charybdis are the two monsters Odysseus and his men have to pass on the way to Ithaka, and the latter is the one that swallows the sea and vomits it back up again.

The Kikonians Character Analysis

Sometimes spelled the Cicones. The resident natives in Ismaros, where Odysseus first lands after leaving Troy. The Ithakans plunder them, because they can, and the Kikonians quite reasonably retaliate, also because they can.

Circe Character Analysis

The sorceress of the island Aiaia.

Ktimene Character Analysis

The daughter of Laertes, Odysseus's sister.

Klytaimestra Character Analysis

Sometimes spelled Clytemnestra. Agamemnon's no-good wife. She sleeps with Aigisthos while her husband is gone and kills Agamemnon when he finally does get home. She meets her death the same way her lover does – at the hands of her and Agamemnon's son Orestes.

Klytoneos Character Analysis

A Phaiakian prince, the son of Alkinoös and Arete. He wins the foot-race during the athletic games, before Odysseus starts throwing his brawn in everyone's face.

Ktesippos Character Analysis

An evil suitor. Pretty much all he does in the *Odyssey* is to throw a cow's foot at beggar Odysseus.

The Cyclopes Character Analysis

Sometimes spelled Cyclopses or Kyklopes. The one-eyed monsters that the Ithakans encounter on the way home.

Laertes Character Analysis

Odysseus's father. For some reason, he seems to live in a shack at the outskirts of Ithaka. Penelope is weaving his funeral shroud.

The Laistrygones Character Analysis

Sometimes spelled Laestrygonians. The scary and not-quite human folk that the Ithakans encounter in Lamos on the way home from Troy. Their king is Antiphates, whom you may remember as the blood-drinking guy.

Laodamas Character Analysis

A Phaiakian prince, the son of Alkinoös and Arete. He wins the boxing match during the athletic games, before Odysseus beats everyone at everything.

Lotus Eaters Character Analysis

The name pretty much says it all. The Lotus Eaters eat the Lotus. Oh, and forget about their lives, homes, families, dreams, and aspirations after doing so. We almost forgot that part.

Maron Character Analysis

The keeper of Apollo's groves at Ismaros; he provides the Ithakans with wine.

Medon Character Analysis

The town crier of Ithaka. He's called out as one of the men loyal to Odysseus, so he accordingly isn't slaughtered along with everyone else in sight.

Melampous Character Analysis

Sometimes spelled Melampus. This is another minor name in a major digression over yet another minor character. Let's see if we can identify some sort of relevance to our tale: In Book XV, Telemachos picks up a hitchhiker fugitive seer on his way back to Ithaka from Sparta. The hitchhiker's name is Theoklymenos, and he is a descendant of Melampous. We then launch into Melampous's story, and find that he was unfairly exiled from his land until he came back and dished up some vengeance, Odysseus-style.

Melanthios Character Analysis

Sometimes spelled Melanthius. The Ithakan goatherd. Unlike many of the other, loyal servants we meet, Melanthios sides with the suitors and insults beggar Odysseus. He's also the one to arm the suitors during the slaughter, but on the other hand he gets tortured before he dies.

Melantho Character Analysis

She's the female version of Melanthios; a servant of the palace who is loyal to the suitors rather than the Queen. She, too, gets her just punishment.

Menelaos Character Analysis

A King of Sparta and husband to Helen; he is the second man Telemachos visits in his search for Odysseus, and it is in fact Menelaos who confirms the boy's father is still alive and on Kalypso's island.

Mentes Character Analysis

Athene first takes the disguise of this man, friend of Odysseus and ruler of the Taphians, when she comes to Ithaka to council Telemachos.

Mentor Character Analysis

Mentor can be confusing in the *Odyssey* since the name either refers to Mentor, the elderly Ithakan, or Mentor, Athene in yet another guise. (Imagine how much easier everyone's life would be if the gods weren't so into these mind-games.)

Mykene Character Analysis

Sometimes spelled Mycenae. Agamemnon's kingdom.

Nausikaa Character Analysis

Sometimes spelled Nausicaa. The Phaiakian princess, daughter of Alkinoös and Arete. Nausikaa is the first of her people to find Odysseus, and it is she who brings him to the palace (somewhat indirectly) to ask for help from the Queen. Her father the King offers her hand in marriage to Odysseus, which might have been nice, had he not been married already.

Neleus Character Analysis

This guy is part of the digression regarding Theoklymenos, the hitchhiking fugitive seer that Telemachos picks up on his way back from Sparta. In the story, Neleus is the not-so-nice King that exiled Melampous, Theoklymenos's ancestor.

Neoptolemos Character Analysis

Also known as Pyrrhus. Achilleus's son. Achilleus asks for him in the Underworld, and Odysseus responds with details of the boy's accomplishments in battles, etc., etc. In other words, the kid brings home a good report card to dad.

Nestor Character Analysis

The King of Pylos and the first man Telemachos goes to visit while searching for news of his father. Nestor provides another great example of good Greek hospitality; plying the Ithakan Prince with gifts, food, and even transportation to his next destination (Sparta). In fact, Pylos is so over-the-top, Telemachos has to bypass his palace on the way back to Ithaka to avoid the time-consuming festivities his return visit would bring.

Noëmon Character Analysis

A wealthy ship-seller in Ithaka. Athene obtains a ship for Telemachos from him.

Orestes Character Analysis

Agamemnon's son; he kills Klytaimestra and her lover Aigisthos as vengeance for his father's death. In the meeting of the gods at the beginning of the *Odyssey*, first on the agenda is murder and whether it was warranted. This is no coincidence. See "Symbols, Imagery, Allegory" for more.

Patroklos Character Analysis

Sometimes spelled Patroclus. One of the shades Odysseus sees in the Underworld. Patroklos was Achilleus's best friend. The *Iliad* tells how, after Patroklos was killed by Hektor, the greatest Trojan warrior, Achilleus swore revenge. He killed Hektor, and thereby sealed his own doom. (To learn more about this, check out our guide to *Iliad* – and then read the book, if you haven't already!)

Peisistratos Character Analysis

Sometimes spelled Peisistratus or Pisistratus. Nestor's son. He accompanies Telemachos to Sparta to see King Menelaos.

Peiraios Character Analysis

One of Telemachos's crewmen. When the Prince comes back to Ithaka at Athene's urging, Peiraios agrees to house Theoklymenos, the hitchhiking fugitive seer they picked up on the way. (More good hospitality, you'll note.)

The Phaiakians Character Analysis

Sometimes spelled the Phaeacians. The hospitable people of Scheria who house Odysseus, listen to his tale, and help him back to Ithaka, only to be destroyed by Poseidon after the fact. These are the people of King Alkinoös, Queen Arete, and the lovely Nausikaa.

Phemios Character Analysis

Sometimes spelled Phemius. The resident bard in Ithaka. We first meet him as he saddens Penelope by singing of the Trojan war. Later, he is spared from the slaughter because he has been loyal to Odysseus during his absence.

Philoitios Character Analysis

A cowherd in Ithaka and one of the servants who remain loyal to Odysseus. He fights on Odysseus's side against the suitors during the slaughter.

Polyphemos Character Analysis

Sometimes spelled Polyphemus. The specific one-eyed monster that the Ithakans encounter on their way home. Unfortunately for everyone involved, Polyphemos eats human flesh. Doubly unfortunately, Polyphemos is Poseidon's son. Once the Greeks blind him and make their escape, Polyphemos calls in a favor from daddy. This means years and years of torture for Odysseus (and his men, until they die). Basically, Polyphemos is the explanation for Poseidon's outrage at Odysseus.

Poseidon Character Analysis

God of the sea, as well as an ever-angry and vengeful grudge-holder. He's the one who forces Odysseus to wander the sea for nearly twenty years, all because the man stabbed his son's eye out and made a big stinkin' deal about it afterwards.

Proteus Character Analysis

An island god we hear about in Menelaos's tale to Telemachos; he reveals to the King how to escape the island he's stuck on (namely, by traveling to Egypt and sacrificing to Zeus).

Euryalos Character Analysis

A Phaiakian who competes in the athletic contests held during Odysseus's stay. He taunts Odysseus about not wanting to take part, leading Odysseus to bust out some top-notch discus-throwing.

The Sirens Character Analysis

These are the dangerous females who lure men to their deaths with their voices. Odysseus becomes the first mortal to have heard their voices and lived to tell the tale when he has his men tie him to the mast yet leave his ears unplugged as they pass.

Skylla Character Analysis

Sometimes spelled Scylla. The first of the two horrible monsters Odysseus must pass with his men (the second is Charybdis). Skylla has six heads and plucks six men from the ship as it passes. Odysseus has been instructed not to try to fight the monster, but rather to row by as quickly as possible. Unfortunately, it takes a good amount of spewing and crunching for him to remember this.

The Taphians Character Analysis

Mentes, the man Athene pretends to be when she first arrives in Ithaka, is the ruler of the Taphians.

Teiresias Character Analysis

Sometimes spelled Tiresias. The blind prophet whose help Odysseus seeks in the Underworld.

Theoklymenos Character Analysis

Sometimes spelled Theoclymenus. The hitchhiker fugitive seer who grabs a ride with Telemachos on his way out of Sparta. A seer is a convenient accessory to have around when there's a slew of omens flying about the place, which happens to be the case in Books XV-XIV.

Character Roles

Protagonist
Odysseus
Odysseus is our hands-down protagonist. For starters, the book is called the *Odyssey*. Homer also makes it explicit that Odysseus is handsome, brave, smart, and an all-around nice guy. Typical classical hero. We also spend the majority of our time following his plotline. We sympathize with him, hate Poseidon for making his life so difficult, and want him to get home already and so he can get rid of all those suitors.

However, Odysseus, like any man (or god, given what we've seen in the *Odyssey*), has flaws – one in particular: *hubris*, or excessive pride. It is this flaw that gets Odysseus into trouble several times with both mortals and immortals, imperils his journey, and complicates his difficulties – but it also makes him human and, in short, an ideal protagonist.

Antagonist

The Suitors (especially Antinoös and Eurymachos)
Throughout the entire epic, the suitors are in the process of eating poor Penelope and Telemachos out of house and home. They transgress all traditional ideas of honor by proposing marriage to a woman still waiting and grieving for her husband. They don't show any respect to the man of the house, Telemachos. They also beat up beggars.

Antagonist

Poseidon
Poseidon is a more conventional antagonist; he has a lot more power than the mortal Odysseus and uses it against him for purposes of vengeance (over that whole Cyclops thing). Poseidon is a more distant villain than the suitors, working his magic from afar and never confronting Odysseus face-to-face for any sort of showdown. Of course, this makes it difficult for Odysseus to best or beat Poseidon in any sort of traditional way; instead, he must make peace with his enemy after suffering the hardship of his punishment.

Guide/Mentor

Athene
Did you notice how Athene takes the disguise of a man named Mentor? No, this wasn't Homer being blatantly obvious – the word "mentor" actually comes from the *Odyssey*. Props to Homer. That means that Athene and the role she plays largely defines what we think if as the Guide or *Mentor* role – the goddess is counselor, champion, cheerleader, and beautician for the mortals she favors.

Foil

Klytaimestra, Aphrodite, and Penelope
These first two women listed are unfaithful wives. We sort of understand Aphrodite's situation because she's the goddess of love. Klytaimestra, on the other hand, is really bad news, as she not only cheated on her husband Agamemnon but killed him when he got back from war. Penelope, however, is a beacon of fidelity. These two adulteresses serve to highlight Penelope's incredible virtue, which makes this a clear foil.

Foil

Odysseus/Telemachos and Agamemnon/Orestes
The foil here is between these two father-son pairs. Agamemnon, as you all know, was killed by his wife and her lover and subsequently avenged by his son Orestes. Odysseus, while not killed, is dishonored and therefore similarly wronged, but in his case only by the suitors (the *potential* lovers of his wife). Telemachos struggles so much throughout the *Odyssey* because of his inability to avenge his father the way Orestes did his. He wants to pay the suitors back for disrespecting the name and property of Odysseus, but finds himself incapable of doing so. The parallel (if minor) story of Agamemnon's death makes palpable for us Telemachos's feelings of obligation.

Character Clues

Epithets
To some extent, Homer tells us what we need to know by, well, just saying it. He beats us over the head with epithets like "clear-headed Telemachos," "wise Penelope," or "Odysseus, master mariner and soldier."

Names
Many characters' names in the *Odyssey* convey important information about their personality or role. Most important of these, of course, is "Odysseus," which the poem ties to the Greek word *odussomai,* which means "to suffer." This connection is made in Book IX, lines 407-409, in the scene where the young Odysseus receives his name from his grandfather, Autolykos. The irony is that, even though Autolykos makes it sound like the name refers to inflicting suffering on others, Odysseus spends much of the poem suffering himself. (Though he sure does inflict a lot of suffering on others too!) The Greeks often portray people as carrying out the will of fate without knowing it. (Just think of the story of Oedipus – or check out our Shmoop guide if you don't know it.) Do you think Autolykos might have been guided by fate in giving Odysseus this name? If so, could be this be part of an argument for exonerating him from responsibility?

Another name that's very important in the *Odyssey* isn't a name at all – that is, "Nobody," the name Odysseus gives to the Cyclops Polyphemos. That was a pretty cool trick, don't you think? At least, that is, until Odysseus's pride gets the better of him and he foolishly tells Polyphemos his real name, and brings down the wrath of Poseidon upon him. OK, but guess what: it's even cooler if you know some tricky stuff that's going on in the Greek. Now, most of this is going to be Greek to you, but just bear with us and we think you'll see how awesome it is. The Greek word for "Nobody" is "outis" (pronounced *OO-tiss*). Now, it just so happens that there's another form of this word (don't worry about why) pronounced "metis" (*MAY-tiss*). So what? Well, it also just so happens that this word "metis" sounds just like a totally different word "metis" (*MAY-tiss*), which means "cleverness." This second word "metis," meaning "cleverness" is very often applied to Odysseus; sometimes he's even called "polymetis," which means something like "clever in many ways."

Coincidence? Not likely. At the most basic level, this is sneaky because when Odysseus is saying that he's "Nobody" – "outis" connected to the first "metis" – he's using his "cleverness" – the second "metis." Then, when he makes the boneheaded move of telling Polyphemos who he is, the stupidity is underlined by the fact that he's no longer "outis"/"metis" and thus no longer acting with his full cleverness. But it actually goes further than that – in ways that you won't have to know Greek to pick up on. Just think back on everything you've read in the poem. How often is Odysseus's cleverness connected with him being nobody, or at least somebody other than himself? That's right, a whole lot of times. Heck, the guy is constantly using his wits to put on various disguises, even pretending to be the lowliest beggar – a "nobody" in a different sense – to achieve his goals.

Among the other names that mean things in the *Odyssey*, you've got "Kalypso," which is related to the Greek word "kalypto" meaning "to hide." This makes sense because, well,

Kalypso *hides* Odysseus on her island for seven years when nobody knows where he is. And the crazy name-games even apply to minor characters, such as "Antinoös," which means "anti-mind," a fitting name for 1) a stupid idiot like Antinoös and 2) a stupid idiot like Antinoös who is enemies with Odysseus, a guy known for cleverness. As for the name of "Phemios" the poet, it is connected to the Greek word "to say." His name is also related to our word "fame" (you get "fame" if people talk about you, right?) even though "fame" comes to us more directly from Latin.

And the list goes on. Unfortunately, we can't go into super detail about the meaning behind every name in the *Odyssey*, but it's good to think about the one's we've given here – especially the ones relating to Odysseus – because they can help you get a new perspective on the poem. The most important take-away, though, is that, in Homer's poem, there's more than meets the eye – and you'd be hard pressed to find something that isn't there for a reason, even if you can't tell what the reason is at first. Is this intimidating? It shouldn't be. It just means that, when you're reading and you notice something interesting, let your brain run with it. You might discover some totally amazing angle on the poem – one that nobody's ever thought of before. (Unless that nobody's Nobody, of course.)

Action
Action is the single most defining sign of a man's character in the *Odyssey*: the suitors show their dishonor by gorging themselves on Odysseus's food and wine without restraint. Odysseus perseveres in his repeated attempts to return home; Telemachos shows his piety by obeying Athene and going on a journey for news of his father; Penelope establishes her faithfulness and virtue by remaining loyal to her husband in his absence.

Sex and Love
This is more to do with women than men in the *Odyssey*, since virtue is a must for females and not so much for males. Compare three women: Penelope, Klytaimestra, and Aphrodite. The first is virtuous because she remains faithful; the second is treacherous because she doesn't (she also murders her husband, which isn't too nice); and the third is humiliated before the other gods for her own sexual impropriety.

Literary Devices

Symbols, Imagery, Allegory

The Sea
Odysseus spends so much time sailing home that the sea really takes up a good chunk of his life. This is fitting, since the sea and its perils work much the same way the *Odyssey* argues that life does; it is full of suffering, but it can't be avoided. The sea can send blessings like sea breezes to blow him home or obstacles like storms, Skylla and Charybdis, and treacherous islands. Because the sea is ruled by Poseidon, it is also a manifestation of the superiority of the gods and nature over man.

Laertes's Shroud

The shroud is a symbol of female deception. Because she is a woman, Penelope doesn't have much power to resist the suitors (as seen repeatedly by her son's commands to go back upstairs to the bedroom, since everything else is a man's affair). So, since she cannot fight them off or throw them out of her house, all she *can* do is delay the day she must pick a suitor. So she stretches that out as far as she can by prolonging the time it takes her to complete an honorable feminine task – weaving a death shroud for the despairing father of Odysseus. Though she spends all day weaving, she unravels her work each night. The fact that Penelope does not actually produce the shroud symbolizes her immobility and her helplessness to make any real progress against her enemy suitors.

Odysseus's Bow

The bow is a symbol of kingship and strength. Whoever strings it is worthy of King Odysseus and can rightfully take the throne. Physical strength was an important quality to the ancient Greeks, not only in warfare, but because psychologically it was tied to political strength and the iron will needed to govern a people who were given to argument and debate.

Not surprisingly, none of the suitors even comes close to succeeding, showing their weakness and folly in vying for Penelope's hand. Telemachos almost strings the bow and might have done it had Odysseus not interrupted him; this shows that Telemachos has matured into manhood and is almost ready to take the place of his father. Of course, that he stops upon request reminds us that he maintains deference to Odysseus's will.

Argos

Odysseus's pet dog is a symbol of unconditional loyalty. Though Argos was a puppy when he last saw Odysseus, many years later he still loves him and shows his affection for his master by wagging his tail and trying to move nearer Odysseus when he hears his voice. Though he is ignored and often mistreated by the hands that once fed him, Argos still hangs around the palace hall, waiting only for his master's return. After seeing him at last, Argos dies happy.

Disguises and Dreams

In the *Odyssey*, disguises are usually a sign of divine intervention, manipulation, and sanction. The gods have no qualms deceiving mortals and helping their favorites deceive others. They often use disguises themselves, reminding us that the gods, too, can be devious. Dreams as well are the direct result of divine power, but tend to be more straightforward and often comfort the sleeping mortal.

Food and Banqueting

In a culture that holds hospitality as an all-important test of character, feasting and festivities are a measure of hospitality and human civility. Often, defects in the banquet signal some fundamental flaw in the host. For example, Polyphemos feasts on human flesh, which makes him, well, an inhuman monster. Circe *seems* hospitable because she serves good food, but proves to be a witch by poisoning that very food with a drug that turns the diners into animals. Odysseus's men transgress boundaries of hospitality by dining on Helios's sacred cattle and suffer death as a consequence. The most obvious example of a misused banquet is the suitors' pillaging of Odysseus's provisions. This shows that the supposedly "noble" men do not have the human qualities of restraint and propriety; they are therefore somewhat less than human

and worthy of death (or so the *Odyssey* argues). On the other hand, Nestor, Menelaos, and the Phaiakians serve proper banquets – full of good food, wine, and singing. They are considered not only good hosts, but great human beings.

Odysseus and Penelope's Bed

It turns out that Odysseus carved his bed from the roots of a live olive tree. As such, the bed is unmovable. It's also growing, but evidently that's not a problem for anyone. The point is that the bed can't be moved, altered, or shaken – it's steadfast and constant, much like the love between this royal couple. Odysseus's sleeping around seems not to count, but Penelope's continuous loyalty is represented by the unmovable bed.

Setting

From Troy in Asia Minor across the islands of the Mediterranean Sea (near Italy) and back to Ithaka, Greece, sometime in the Bronze Age.

Much of the action in the *Odyssey* takes place on the sea, where Odysseus must battle against the storms of the sea god, Poseidon, but the last third of the story is set in the town and countryside of Ithaka. The setting is a geographical potpourri of what was important, mythologically, in Homer's time period. Scholars have tried to correlate various places in the *Odyssey* with real locations in the Mediterranean, but there's a lot of guess work involved in this. It's very possible that Homer based his hero's wanderings on real geography but extrapolated and manipulated to suit his narrative purposes. Anyway, enough about that: here's a list for you.

Aiaia (Aeaea): The island home of one Circe, everyone's favorite sorceress.

Aiolia: The island ruled by Aiolos, god of the winds.

Elysion: The *Odyssey*'s version of a heavenly afterlife.

Ithaka: You know what Ithaka is. And how Odysseus made it home there by the longest route ever.

Ismaros: The first place Odysseus and his men land after leaving Troy. This is the land of the Kikonians, whom the Ithakans plunder until driven from their shores.

Lakedaimon: Another name for Sparta. (Technically, this refers to the surrounding area of which Sparta is the capital.)

Lamos: The land of the Laistrygones, the giant/ogres/weirdos, and King Antiphates, drinker of blood. Needless to say, Odysseus and the Ithakans leave this place pretty quickly. Well, except for that one guy who was chugged by Antiphates.

Mount Parnassos (Parnassus): Where Odysseus goes hunting with his uncle when he's a

little boy. This is where the boar/thigh-scar incident took place.

Mount Olympos (Olympus): The gods' hangout/home/pad.

Ogygia: Kalypso's island, where Odysseus is held for seven years.

Pherai: Telemachos and Peisistratos spend the night here on the way to Pylos from Sparta.

Pylos: The first place Telemachos travels in his search for news of his father. Here he dines with King Nestor and his son Peisistratos before leaving for Menelaos in Sparta.

Scheria: The island of the Phaiakians. This is Odysseus's last stop before he reaches Ithaka and also the location where he tells his tale.

Thrinakia (Thrinacia or Trinacria): The land where the sun god Helios keeps his super-duper cattle.

The Underworld: The land of the dead. Odysseus travels here to speak with Teiresias, the dead, blind prophet. While there, he converses with many other "shades," including his war buddies and his mother.

Narrator Point of View

First Person (Peripheral Narrator) or Third Person (Omniscient), depending on how technical you want to get; First Person (Central Narrator) is used in the parts told by Odysseus.

Homer, the poet, shows us everything that happens in the *Odyssey*. The narration appears to be in the third person unless you consider Homer's invocation to the Muse in Book I in which he uses personal pronouns and references himself telling the story. Of course, you could write this off as a standard introduction, not as part of the poem itself, in which case Third Person Omniscient is the label you want. Either way, practically speaking, the poem reads like a third person tale, usually vocalized through Odysseus or Telemachos, because Homer is not a character and does not take part in the action.

In Books IX – XII, Odysseus becomes the narrator and tells the story in the first person, which allows us greater insight into the psychology of his character. We get to see how he views his experiences, whether or not he has learned from them (for instance, does he tell his stories with a sense of reflection and wisdom?), and whether he still suffers from certain key flaws (does he tell his story with an excessive measure of pride?). And importantly, this narrative tactic works for Homer structurally; it allows him to deliver the story of the *Odyssey* out of its proper chronological order; he gets to jump right in to the middle of the action when the epic begins.

Genre

Epic Poetry; Folklore, Legend, and Mythology; Quest

Along with Homer's *Iliad*, the *Odyssey* is one of the two great epics of ancient Greece. Actually, they sort of defined what an epic was in the first place. Both poems display many of the epic's characteristics, featuring a larger than life hero, deeds of great valor, and the interference of the gods in human affairs. Also, both poems use literary devices that have become typical of epics: opening with an invocation to the muse; beginning the story *in medias res* (basically, "in the middle of things"); providing long lists of people, genealogies, and places significant to mythological history; and using epithets, or repeated nicknames, for various characters, major and minor. For the Ancient Greeks, it was also important that an epic be written in the poetic meter of "dactylic hexameter" (see our "Writing Style" section for details) – which both the *Iliad* and the *Odyssey* are.

On the other hand, it's important to remember that the *Iliad* was probably composed first, so you can see the *Odyssey* playing around a bit with the pattern the earlier epic established. It does this by having a more complicated plot; by including characters from lower social orders (such as Eumaios the swineherd); and by having much of the action centered around women in the home. This is probably connected with the fact that parts of the story (especially the parts recounted by Odysseus) resemble cultural folklore, involving unrealistic, mythological creatures and occurrences. These render it a player in the mythology genre and, of course, a major example of a quest (basically, a hero facing obstacles on his way to get somewhere).

Tone

Serious, Humorous

Homer writes with a great sense of gravity that you would pretty much expect when reading about epic heroes and their long dangerous journeys. These matters, although they may seem outlandish to us, are taken very seriously: Odysseus's suffering is palpable and never seems to end; Penelope's longing for her husband is evident in her many tears; Telemachos journeys far and risks his life to find out news of his father; and even the gods gravely consider the plight of the mortals below.

At the same time, there is comic relief in some of the stories about the gods (like Demodokos singing about how Hephaistos caught wife, Aphrodite, with Ares); in the banter between servants; and in the tricks played by Odysseus and Athene. If there's one single metaphor for this balancing act between tones, it comes when Homer compares Odysseus stringing his bow to a singer tuning his lyre (Book XXI, lines 404-411). The *Odyssey* is just like that: delicately – perhaps dangerously – poised between something harsh and warlike (the bow), yet also beautiful and enchanting (the lyre).

Writing Style

Clear, Poetic

OK, now we know what you're thinking: how could we possibly think the language of the *Odyssey* is clear? When you start reading Homer, you're probably going to think his way of saying things is pretty weird and formal – at any rate, far from clear. (We know because we sure felt this way our first time picking it up.) The thing is, you have to look at Homeric style as a little bit like learning a new dialect. It won't take you long to get the hang of it – maybe the first few books or so – but once you do, you're home free, because it falls into a very regular pattern, with a lot of repetitions. Once you get past the initial strangeness, you'll see that Homer's work is almost never complicated for its own sake. He just says things in a very clear and direct way – in his own distinctive language.

Homeric Simile

As for our calling it poetic, we know this might just seem redundant. It *is* a poem after all. But *because* of that, it's important to recognize the distinctive features of Homer's poetic style. Probably the most famous of these is the so-called "Homeric simile." A simile, in case you don't remember, is a way of describing something by explicitly comparing it to something else: "A is like B." Homer's distinctive way of making similes comes up more often in the *Iliad* than the *Odyssey*, but there are still some famous examples of it spicing up Odysseus's (already very spicy) adventures.

One famous example appears in Book VI, lines 130-136. It follows the three-step process of your typical Homeric simile: 1) saying what it is that whatever you're talking about is like (in this case, Odysseus is like a lion); 2) describing the thing you're comparing it to (the lion); and 3) reminding the audience of what you were originally talking about (Odysseus). The third step is important because sometimes the description the second step can get extremely long, and there's the risk that the audience will forget what you're talking about.

Dactylic Hexameter

The final important thing we should point out in Homer's style is his meter: the tongue-twisting "dactylic hexameter." Try saying that five times fast. Or wait, make that *six* times. Why six times? Well, here's the deal. Even though they look like syllable soup, the two words "dactylic" and "hexameter" actually mean something. Just to be tricky, let's start with "hexameter."

The "hex" in "hexameter" is the same as in "hexagon," which you might remember is a six-sided shape. And the "meter" part is like…well, "meter," a unit of measurement. So a "hexameter" is a poetic meter with six measures. (We're using "measures" here in the musical sense, meaning the same thing as "bars.") Because measures or bars in poetry are known as feet, you might as well just translate "hexameter" as "six feet."

OK, but what about the "dactylic" part? This comes from the Greek word "daktylos," which means "finger." We might as well just translate "dactylic" as "fingery." So far so good? Good. Now take a look at your finger – any finger except for your thumb. You will probably notice that it has one long joint followed by two short joints. That's the basic idea the Greeks were trying to

get across in calling this meter dactylic – are you ready for this? It's made up of *FEET* that are shaped like *FINGERS*: one long syllable followed by two short syllables.

From what we've already learned about the word "hexameter," can you guess how many of such feet are going to be in a line? If you guessed "six," give yourself a pat on the back: you are *almost* completely right. Why "almost"? That's because, in dactylic hexameter, only the first *five* feet are shaped like fingers (LONG + short + short); the last foot is never shaped this way; it will be either: (LONG + LONG) or (LONG + short). To illustrate this meter in action, let's just take our handy-dandy translations, "fingery" (LONG + short + short) and "six feet" (LONG-short):

"Fingery | fingery | fingery | fingery | fingery | six-feet"

Pretty neat, huh? Of course, thousands and thousands of lines in that rhythm would start to get pretty annoying, so the ancients allowed you to plug in a (LONG + LONG) in exchange for any one of the first five feet. (This usually happened in only the first four.) This allowed a wide range of rhythms to achieve a variety of poetic effects and keep things interesting. Unfortunately, this meter does not come through in English translations of the work, though some translations – such as Richmond Lattimore – try to replicate some of its features in their English lines. Other translations, such as Robert Fitzgerald, just switch to the most tried-and-true of English poetic meters: the iambic pentameter.

What's Up With the Title?

"The Odyssey" is a form of the hero (Odysseus's) name and basically means "the story of Odysseus." The *Odyssey* has become so famous that the word "odyssey" has a place in the English lexicon and has come to mean any epic voyage.

What's Up With the Ending?

For a long time, some readers have felt that the ending of the *Odyssey* smells a little fishy. In fact, two scholars from ancient Alexandria (Aristarchus and Aristophanes – a different Aristophanes than the one who wrote comedic plays) claimed that the "ending" of the *Odyssey* came in line 296 – of Book XXIII! According to these wise guys, everything after Odysseus and Penelope go to bed together – including all of Book XXIV – was added later by somebody other than Homer. Why would they think that? Your guess is as good as ours, though plenty of later scholars have tried to back them up, arguing that Book XXIV isn't of the same quality as the rest of the *Odyssey*, and so on. Now, it may be true that the ending is a bit abrupt – just when a big battle is about to pit Odysseus, Telemachos, and Laertes against the families of the dead suitors, Athena steps in and tells everybody to be friends. (Thundering from Zeus drives the point home)

That said, there's a lot of important stuff in Book XXIV that you can't really do without. Most important of all is Odysseus's reunion with his father Laertes. We've been hearing about Laertes throughout the whole book – remember, the shroud Penelope is weaving is going to be for him when he dies – and it wouldn't make sense for Homer just to forget about him. Also, in

Ancient Greek culture, where honor and revenge were very important (check out the *Iliad* for further examples of this), it simply wouldn't make sense to end the poem with a bunch of guys still out to get Odysseus. This is especially true given that, in lines 113-140 of Book XXIII – before the line that Aristarchus and Aristophanes claim is the end of the poem – Odysseus and Telemachos discuss the problem of the suitors' families and decide to go hide out in the country with Laertes. Was Homer just going to leave that thread hanging? We at Shmoop think it's more likely that *any* ending would have seemed abrupt after a poem as awesome as the *Odyssey*. What was most important for the poet was wrapping everything up peacefully, even if it did require divine intervention.

Did You Know?

Trivia

- The first four books of the *Odyssey* are sometimes known as the "Telemachy" because they revolve around (guess who) Telemachos. (Source: Bertman, Stephen. "The Telemachy and Structural Symmetry." *Transactions and Proceedings of the American Philological Association* 97 (1966): 15-27.)
- For a long time, people have debated whether the last book of the *Odyssey* was written by Homer. There is speculation that it might have been added by another poet, mostly because the quality doesn't match that of the first two. (Source)
- Classics scholar Martin West has argued that the *Odyssey* was heavily influenced by the Sumerian poem the *Epic of Gilgamesh*. (Source)
- Many scholars think that the *Odyssey* had a long and rich oral tradition before ever being written down. Homer's epithets, repeated phrases, and metrical idiosyncrasies all functioned as mnemonic devices for those bards and singers who memorized the verse and passed it down from generation to generation. That's why you see some of the same phrases over and over – like "But when the young dawn showed again with her rosy fingers." In Greek, this is a stock phrase that fits the meter of the poem. Think of it as a go-to line for the oral poets. (Source)
- The Canadian poet and novelist Margaret Atwood wrote a book called *The Penelopiad*. (Source)
- Nobel Prize-winning poet Derek Walcott wrote a long poem entitled *Omeros* which used Homeric themes to depict life in his native St. Lucia – and island in the Caribbean.
- In addition to the poem " Ulysses," the nineteenth-century English poet Alfred Lord Tennyson also wrote a poem about the Lotus Eaters, which stretches that brief moment in Homer's text like a piece of silly-putty. You can read the poem here.
- The opening poem of the epic *Cantos* by modernist poet Ezra Pound is a quirky translation of the decent to the Underworld in Book XI of the *Odyssey*. You can read Pound's weird version here; part of the strangeness might be explained by the fact that he was working, not from the Greek, but from a sixteenth-century Latin version by Andreas Divus – as he reveals at the end of his translation.
- The Modern Greek poet Cavafy wrote a poem based on Odysseus's travels entitled "Ithaca," which you can read here.

- The English-American poet Thom Gunn wrote a poem about the transformations brought on by Circe (and, indirectly, of the transformations brought on by LSD), and named it after "moly," the weird plant that Hermes gives to Odysseus to keep him safe. Read the poem here.
- "Moly" also features prominently in this lecture by the Canadian poet and classics scholar Anne Carson, in which she talks about issues of translation – and what to do with words that can't be translated. You can read her thoughts on the matter here.
- Pulitzer Prize-winning American poet Stephen Dunn wrote a poem about Odysseus. And you can find it in his book *Different Hours*.

Steaminess Rating

R

Odysseus is quite the player, what with the all ladies and the all goddesses he sleeps with. Seven whole years with Kalypso? It's distinctly possible that Odysseus spent more years with her than he did with his wife Penelope to begin with. There was also Circe, who wanted Odysseus so badly that she reversed all her magic to get him. Nausikaa also has a crush on our hero, but he doesn't seem too interested, maybe because she's too young. And despite the many affairs, Odysseus returns home to his still-faithful bride for a lovely romantic reunion.

Allusions and Cultural References

Literature, Philosophy, and Mythology

- Homer : the *Iliad* – By nature of repeated references to previous events that are detailed in Homer's earlier poem. Here are a few examples: Achilleus (3.114), The Trojan horse (8.533-558), Helen (23.246-252), Achilleus and Agamemnon (24.16-111)

Best of the Web

Movie or TV Productions
1992-1994 TV Series
http://imdb.com/title/tt0103504/
The Odyssey is a spin-off on Homer's epic poem about a man in a coma.

1987 Animated TV Movie
http://imdb.com/title/tt0821800/
This Australian animated movie doesn't have very good reviews.

1997 TV Movie
http://imdb.com/title/tt0118414/
In this TV movie version of the *Odyssey* Armand Assante plays Odysseus, Isabella Rossellini acts as Athene, and Vanessa Williams is Kalypso.

2000 Movie
http://imdb.com/title/tt0190590/
O Brother, Where Art Thou? is a modernized spin-off on the *Odyssey* directed by the Coen brothers and starring George Clooney.

2004 Movie
http://imdb.com/title/tt0332452/
Troy is a movie about the Trojan war, the war that Odysseus left home to fight in. Odysseus is played by Sean Bean.

1967 Movie
http://imdb.com/title/tt0062414/
Ulysses, directed by Joseph Strick is based on the James Joyce novel. Ulysses another name for Odysseus.

2006 TV Series
http://imdb.com/title/tt0758577/
Class of the Titans, directed by Brad Goodchild, has a character named Odie Star based on Odysseus.

1981 Animated TV Movie
http://imdb.com/title/tt0131190/
Ulysses 31, directed by Bernard Deyriès and Kyosuke Mikuriya, is a Franco-Japanese anime production.

1979 Documentary
http://imdb.com/title/tt0488271/
Unterwegs mit Odysseus, directed by Tony Munzlinger, is a German documentary tracing the sites of Odysseus's journey.

Audios

Modern-Day Soldiers Relate to the *Odyssey*
http://www.npr.org/templates/player/mediaPlayer.html?action=1&t=1&islist=false&id=14682035&m=14673994
Genius Grant recipient Dr. Jonathan Shay discusses the relevance of the *Odyssey* to American soldiers returning home from the war in Iraq. NPR *Morning Edition*.

Cream
http://www.youtube.com/watch?v=u8hLc_nqx8g
"Tales of Brave Ulysses" by Cream.

Videos
The Police
http://www.youtube.com/watch?v=aw1MNBgLw0w
"King of Pain" by The Police…this song refers to Odysseus.

Images
Odyssey Written on Papyrus
http://www.metmuseum.org/toah/hd/ipha/ho_09.182.50.htm
The Metropolitan Museum of Art displays an early Hellenistic Papyrus fragment with lines from Homer's *Odyssey*.

Greek Vase
http://www.perseus.tufts.edu/cgi-bin/image?lookup=1993.01.0608&type=vase
The image on this vase depicts Odysseus coming up against the Sirens.

Odysseus
http://www.perseus.tufts.edu/cgi-bin/image?lookup=1992.06.1537&type=vase
An ancient image of Odysseus.

Odyssey-Related Art
http://www.perseus.tufts.edu/cgi-bin/image?lookup=1991.01.0287&type=vase
A painting of Odysseus and Circe.

Another Vase
http://www.perseus.tufts.edu/cgi-bin/image?lookup=1993.01.0668&type=vase
This vase has a picture of Odysseus getting his feet washed.

Odysseus Painting
http://www.perseus.tufts.edu/cgi-bin/image?lookup=1993.01.0348&type=vase
Odysseus in the Underworld chatting with Teiresias.

Odysseus Painting
http://www.perseus.tufts.edu/cgi-bin/image?lookup=1991.10.0965&type=vase
Odysseus hanging on to the bottom of a sheep.

More Sheep
http://www.perseus.tufts.edu/cgi-bin/image?lookup=1990.14.0148&type=vase
Another vase with Odysseus tied to the underside of a sheep.

Yet Another Vase
http://www.perseus.tufts.edu/cgi-bin/image?lookup=1993.01.0656&type=vase
This one has a picture of Odysseus slaying all of the suitors.

Penelope and Telemachus
http://www.perseus.tufts.edu/cgi-bin/image?lookup=1993.01.0667&type=vase
This vase shows Penelope sitting at her loom next to her son.

Ancient Art
http://www.perseus.tufts.edu/cgi-bin/image?lookup=1990.34.0552&type=vase
Odysseus and Nausicaa on…another vase.

Documents

"Ancient sarcophagus unearthed in Cyprus"
http://www.usatoday.com/tech/science/discoveries/2006-03-20-sarcophagus-find_x.htm
In 2006, construction workers in western Cyprus discovered a 2,500-year-old sarcophagus (coffin) with color illustrations of Homer's epics, including the *Odyssey*.

In case you can read Greek…
http://www.library.northwestern.edu/homer/html/application.html
…here's a copy of the original Greek text.

A Full Translation of the *Odyssey*
http://classics.mit.edu/Homer/odyssey.9.ix.html
No matter which translation you're using, it's always convenient to have another translation nearby in case one section is particularly confusing. Also, two is always better than one. This is a really straightforward, simply-translated prose version of the *Odyssey* from some scholars at MIT. You can also read another one at the same website (The Chicago Homer) that has the text in Greek.

"Odysseus' Scar"
http://www.westmont.edu/~fisk/Articles/OdysseusScar.html
To escape persecution because he was Jewish, the German literary scholar Erich Auerbach fled to Istanbul, Turkey, where he remained for the duration of WWII. While he was there, with only access to a limited number of books, he wrote a famous work of literary criticism entitled *Mimesis: A History of the Representation of Reality in Western Literature*. The first chapter of the book, which is itself very famous, is called "Odysseus' Scar"; in it, Auerbach compares the narrative techniques of Homer with those of the Bible. Even though most scholars now think that Auerbach's presentation of Homer is too simplistic, his essay still offers many interesting insights. You can read it here

Websites

Odyssey Jeopardy
http://jc-schools.net/tutorials/Eng9/odysseygame1.ppt
Jefferson County Schools has created a terrific "Jeopardy" style trivia game for students to study the *Odyssey*. Categories include "Gods and Goddesses." "Mere Mortals," "Monsters," "Travel and Tourism," and "Misc." (Linked file is in PowerPoint.)

Odyssey GoogleLitTrip
http://www.googlelittrips.com/GoogleLit/9-12/Entries/2006/9/15_The_Odyssey_by_Homer.html

GoogleLit Trips is a website devoted to helping teachers and students explore literature by using Google Earth. Check out this Google Earth map of Homer's travels

Map of the Odyssey
http://danp.us/gallery/odyssey_map.jpg
Maps are tricky when it comes to the *Odyssey*, since Homer probably was working from geography but probably not always true to it. Still, here's a rough idea of where some of Odysseus's episodes may have taken place.

Another Map
http://nadabs.tripod.com/odyssey/mainmap.gif
Here's another take on the geographical locations of Odysseus's travels.

Greek Mythology
http://www.theoi.com/
Need to brush up on your Greek mythology? This is the site for you.

Printed in Great Britain
by Amazon

37833569R00081